INTRODU

GW01237052

WORD Processing

INTRODUCING

WORD

Processing

Exam success at Stage I

Carol McKenzie

Pat Bryden

Heinemann Educational
a division of Heinemann Publishers (Oxford) Ltd,
Halley Court, Jordan Hill, Oxford OX2 8EJ

OXFORD LONDON EDINBURGH MADRID ATHENS BOLOGNA
PARIS MELBOURNE SYDNEY AUCKLAND SINGAPORE TOKYO
IBADAN NAIROBI HARARE GABORONE PORTSMOUTH NH (USA)

© Carol McKenzie and Pat Bryden 1994

First published 1994

95 96 97 10 9 8 7 6 5 4 3

A catalogue record for this book is available from the British Library on request.

ISBN 0 435 453009

Designed by Ken Vail Graphic Design, Cambridge using Quark XPress 3.1™
on the Apple Mackintosh™ Ci

Printed in Great Britain by Henry Ling Ltd, at the Dorset Press, Dorchester, Dorset

Acknowledgements
The authors and publishers would like to thank the RSA for permission to
reproduce examination requirements and the list of standard abbreviations.

Contents

Contents

The first part of the book is designed for students preparing to take the RSA CLAIT (Computer Literacy And Information Technology) Application in Word Processing. All the objectives for meeting the CLAIT word-processing requirements are covered in Units 1–7.

These units are also suitable for beginners who wish to learn basic word-processing skills or prepare themselves for the RSA Core Text or RSA Stage I Word Processing examination.

Units 1–7

These units cover CLAIT Word Processing profile sentences:

- Switch on and load a word-processing system and enter text.
- Insert, delete and move text; replace words.
- Change margins, line spacing and justification; embolden and centre text.
- Save text and print; exit from system with data secure.

You should already have had instruction on using a QWERTY keyboard and a printer.

Assessment

At the end of Unit 7 you should be able to complete a CLAIT word-processing assignment:

a within approximately two hours (this is a guide only – there is no time limit)

b with no more than three data-entry errors

c with *no errors* in system/program manipulation.

After Unit 7

Units 8–13 are designed for students preparing to take the RSA Core Text Processing Skills examination using a word-processing program. All the points of theory required for this examination are covered in Units 8–13.

After completing Unit 13, you may progress to Units 14–21 to cover the theory for the RSA I Word Processing examination. You will derive most benefit from this book by working through the units in the order they appear. It has been designed to be a progressive course.

Note: Do not delete any files from your disk as some of these will be required to complete later units.

Before attempting Units 8–21 you *must* already have completed the previous units in this book *or* covered theory on:

- keying in text
- moving cursor around the document
- editing text (i.e., inserting/deleting characters, lines, paragraphs, splitting and joining paragraphs)
- saving, printing and retrieving files
- changing margin settings and line spacing.

Assessment

At the end of Unit 13 you should be able to complete the RSA Core Text Processing Skills examination:

a   within a one-hour time limit

b   with no more than 45 accuracy and 15 presentation errors for an award with 'Pass'

c   with no more than 15 accuracy and 9 presentation errors for an award with 'Distinction'.

At the end of Unit 21 you should be able to complete the RSA I Word Processing examination:

a   within a one-and-a-half-hour time limit

b   with no more than seven accuracy and five presentation errors for an award with 'Pass'

c   with no more than two accuracy and two presentation errors for an award with 'Distinction'.

Symbols

When you see this symbol, read all the information before you begin.

When you see this symbol, carry out the exercises.

At the end of Unit 1 you will have learned how to:

a   load your word-processing program
b   select correct disk drive for working on
c   create a document/file
d   key in text
e   move the cursor around a document
f   edit text – delete/insert character(s)/word(s)
g   split/join paragraphs
h   save work to disk
i   print work
j   clear the screen
k   exit from the word-processing program.

Follow the instructions step by step.

SWITCH ON AND LOAD WP PROGRAM	**1.1** Switch on and load your word-processing program.
CHANGE LOGGED DISK DRIVE TO A	**1.2** Make sure that you are working on the correct disk drive so that your work will be saved on to your personal disk, usually in drive A.
CREATE A NEW DOCUMENT	**1.3** You are going to create a new document called **Unit1**. Some programs require a document to be named and opened *before* keying in, others allow naming to take place *after* keying in when saving the file. Use the method appropriate to the program you are using.

Key in text

Wordwrap	When you key in text, you do not need to press ⏎ at the end of each line as your word-processing program will automatically do this for you. (This is called wordwrap.)
Initial capitals	To type an initial capital (first letter of a word): **Press:** Shift key + letter
Closed capitals	**Press:** Caps lock key (to start typing in capitals). Press again to end capitals.
Clear lines	To leave a blank line between paragraphs. **Press:** ⏎ twice (at end of each paragraph) *Note:* You should leave at least one clear line space after headings. You should leave one clear line space between paragraphs and different parts of a document.
Punctuation **full stop**	No space before, one or two spaces after – be consistent.
comma	No space before, one space after.
question/exclamation	Same as full stop because they are used at the end of a sentence.
colon (:)	No space before; two spaces after when followed by a capital letter; one space after when followed by a lower-case letter.
semi-colon (;)	No space before, one space after.
brackets and single/ double quotation marks	One space before the opening sign; one space after the closing sign; no spaces immediately inside the signs.

Exercise 1A

1.4   Refer to the information section: 'Key in text'. Key in the following text–do not worry if you make mistakes, you can correct them later!

```
INTRODUCTION TO WORD PROCESSING

Word Processing is sometimes called Text Processing but the latter
term is usually used to cover not only Word Processing but also
Typewriting and Audio Transcription.

This book has been designed to allow you to achieve the skills you
need to be successful in RSA (Royal Society of Arts) examinations.
You can work at your own pace at home, in a school or college, or
at work.  Print-out checks are provided at the back of the book so
that you can be sure your work is correct before you go on to the
next section.  It is recommended that you work through the book
step-by-step so that your skills increase and develop in a logical
manner.

Before commencing a Text Processing course, it is important that
you can use a QWERTY keyboard reasonably well.  Learning the
correct fingering methods first means that you will be able to
become a fast and accurate Text Processor operator.

This book is designed for use with any Text Processing program and
space has been left at relevant points for the insertion of the
specific program commands.
```

1.5   Practise moving the cursor around the document you have just keyed in:

- move the cursor left word by word
- move the cursor right word by word
- move the cursor to the end of a line
- move the cursor to the start of a line
- move the cursor to the top of the document
- move the cursor to the bottom of the document.

CURSOR MOVEMENT

1.6   Proofread your work very carefully.

1.7 Edit the passage as shown below:

- delete any words crossed out
- insert text at points marked ⋏
- make new paragraphs at all the points marked ⌐
- join the paragraphs at the run-on ↪ sign
- in the last two paragraphs, change the word **Text** to **Word** using the overtype method.

Your name

INTRODUCTION TO WORD PROCESSING

Word Processing is sometimes called Text Processing but the latter term is usually used to cover not only Word Processing but also Typewriting and Audio Transcription.

This book has been designed to allow you *(the student)* to achieve the skills ~~you need~~ to be successful in RSA (Royal Society of Arts) examinations. You can work at your own pace at home, in a school or college, or at work. Print-out checks are provided at the back of the book so that you can be sure your work is correct before you go on to the next ~~section~~ *unit*. It is recommended that you work through the book step-by-step *(so that your skills and knowledge increase)* and develop in a logical manner. *(Don't forget to use them.)*

Before commencing a Text Processing course, it is important that you can use a QWERTY keyboard ~~reasonably~~ well. Learning the correct fingering methods first means that you will *later* be able to become a fast and accurate Text Processor operator.

This book is designed for use with any Text Processing program and space has been left at relevant points for the insertion of the specific program commands. *Refer to your Manufacturer's manual or your tutor for help.*

1.8 Compare your work on screen with the print-out check at the back of the book. Proofread carefully and make any necessary amendments.

1.9 **Save** your file – use the filename **EX1A**.

1.10 When your document is perfect, **print** a copy of your work.

1.11 **Clear** the screen (if necessary).

1.12 **Exit** the program if you have finished working, or continue straight on to the next unit.

EDIT TEXT – DELETE AND INSERT

PARAGRAPHS – SPLIT/JOIN

SAVE WORK TO DISK

PRINT OUT HARD COPY

CLEAR THE SCREEN

EXIT THE PROGRAM

At the end of Unit 2 you will have learned how to:

a   retrieve a file from disk
b   shade (highlight) a block of text
c   delete a block of text
d   restore deleted text
e   move a block of text
f   copy a block of text
g   insert a paragraph.

Follow the instructions step by step.

RETRIEVE A FILE FROM DISK

2.1   Display on screen the list, or directory, of files on your work disk. Retrieve the file you saved in Unit 1 (filename **EX1A**).

SHADE A BLOCK OF TEXT

When you want to change a block of text in some way, it is usually necessary first of all to mark, highlight or 'shade' the particular section of text. Move the cursor to the first character of the text to be shaded and then follow the instructions for shading.

In Unit 1 you learnt how to delete individual words. It would be too time consuming to delete larger portions of text in the same way. You should 'shade' the block of text you wish to delete and then operate the command(s) for deletion.

DELETE A BLOCK OF TEXT

RESTORE DELETED TEXT

If you delete text accidentally or change your mind you can usually restore it provided that you do so straightaway.

If you decide that a particular section of text needs to be moved, you can do this quickly without deleting and retyping. Move the cursor to the first character of the block of text to be moved and shade the block. Follow the instructions for moving a block of text.

MOVE A BLOCK OF TEXT

Copying a block of text means that the text will remain in its original place in the document and a *copy* of the same text will also appear elsewhere. Move the cursor to the first character of the block of text to be copied and shade the block. Follow the instructions for copying a block of text.

COPY A BLOCK OF TEXT

Exercise 2A

2.2   Rearrange the passage as shown opposite:

● **Delete** paragraph A (follow instructions 'Shade a block of text' and 'Delete a block of text').

● **Restore** paragraph A (follow instructions 'Restore deleted text').

● **Delete** the circled words in paragraph B (follow instructions 'Shade a block of text' and 'Delete a block of text').

● **Move** paragraph D so it appears under paragraph B (follow instructions 'Move a block of text' and remember to leave one clear line above and below each paragraph).

● **Copy** the heading **introduction to word processing** to E (follow instructions 'Copy a block of text' – leave one clear line after last paragraph).

```
Your name

INTRODUCTION TO WORD PROCESSING
```

(A) Word Processing is sometimes called Text Processing but the latter term is usually used to cover not only Word Processing but also Typewriting and Audio Transcription.

(B) This book has been designed to allow you (the student) to achieve the skills to be successful in RSA (Royal Society of Arts) examinations.

(C) You can work at your own pace at home, in a school or college, or at work. Print-out checks are provided at the back of the book so that you can be sure your work is correct before you go on to the next unit. Don't forget to use them. It is recommended that you work through the book step-by-step so that your skills and knowledge increase and develop in a logical manner.

(D) Before commencing a Word Processing course, it is important that you can use a QWERTY keyboard well. Learning the correct fingering methods first means that you will later be able to become a fast and accurate Word Processor operator. This book is designed for use with any Word Processing program and space has been left at relevant points for the insertion of the specific program commands. Refer to your Manufacturer's manual or your tutor for help.

(E) *

2.3 You are now going to insert a new paragraph into the document. Move the cursor to the beginning of the second paragraph–the one beginning **This book has been** …

```
Press: ⤺ twice (to insert two blank lines)

Press: ↑ twice

Insert the following paragraph:
```

```
Word Processing is not only an updated method of producing
documents.  It is more than an extension of typewriting.
Nowadays many executives and administrators do their own word
processing so that they can compose on to the screen and
produce perfect copy in a short time.
```

2.4 Make sure there is one clear blank line above and below the paragraph you have just inserted.

2.5 Compare your work on screen with the print-out check at the back of the book. Proofread carefully and make any necessary amendments.

2.6 Save your file – use the filename **EX2A**.

2.7 When your document is perfect, print a copy of your work.

2.8 Exit the program if you have finished working, or continue straight on to the next unit.

Change the document format, margins and line spacing

At the end of Unit 3, you will have learned how to change the document format in the following ways:

a   ragged right margin
b   justified right margin
c   inset left margin
d   inset right margin
e   double-line spacing
f   view (preview) a document before printing.

Follow the instructions step by step.

3.1   Retrieve the document you saved at the end of Unit 2 if it is not already on your screen. The filename is **EX2A**.

Right margin–ragged or justified

Look at the document on your screen. The left margin is straight, but the right margin is 'ragged' (the lines do not end at the same point).   } Ragged right margin

In word processing you can adjust the text so that the right margin is also quite straight as shown in this paragraph. This is called a 'justified' right margin (all the lines end at exactly the same point).   } Justified right margin

It is normal practice to use either a justified right margin or a ragged right margin for a document.

Your program may be set 'by default' to a ragged or a justified right margin. Check the default settings of the program you are using. The default setting may be changed.

It is important that the cursor is positioned correctly before inserting the ragged or justified margin command. This is usually at the top of the document or immediately above the block of text to be altered.

RAGGED RIGHT MARGIN

JUSTIFIED RIGHT MARGIN

In some programs, a justified right margin does not show on the screen and you may have to view the document to check. The view (or preview) function is covered later in this unit.

Inset left/right margins

In word processing you can format (adjust) the text so that portions of your document are *set in* from either margin.

> This method of emphasis is often used to draw the reader's attention to a particular piece of information–like this!

Inset text

On most programs, the left and right margins are preset at 10 characters (or 1 inch). *If you are using a 10-pitch font, 10 characters = 1 inch.* This means that, even if the text appears to fill the VDU screen, there will be a left and right margin of 1 inch on the page when it is printed.

Your program may use characters or inches as units of measurement. Find out about this in your program. These default settings may be changed.

Before changing a margin setting, make sure that the cursor is in the correct position – where you want new settings to begin.

After changing a margin setting, you may need to move the cursor to the end of the document so that the typing lines will reformat to the new margins. (On some programs, it is necessary to use a 'format' or 'reformat' function.)

Examples

To inset margins by 1 inch at left and right margins, add 10 (characters) or 1 inch to the existing settings, thus changing them to 20 characters (or 2 inches).
To inset margins by ¹/₂ inch at left and right margins, add 5 (characters) or ¹/₂ inch to the existing settings, thus changing them to 15 characters (or 1.5 inch).

MARGINS (TO CHANGE)

Double-line spacing

In word processing you can format (adjust) the text so that portions of your document appear in double-line spacing (i.e., one blank line between each line of text):

> This is another method of emphasis used to highlight a
>
> particular portion of text – like this!

Double-line space

Position the cursor where you want double-line spacing to start before inserting the command.

DOUBLE-LINE SPACING

If you experience problems, check whether your program can do double-line spacing, and whether it will show on screen.

Exercise 3A

3.2 Reformat the passage as shown below—refer to the instructions for reformatting text:

Your name

Use a ragged right margin

INTRODUCTION TO WORD PROCESSING

Inset L & R margins by ½"

double spacing

Word Processing is sometimes called Text Processing but the latter term is usually used to cover not only Word Processing but also Typewriting and Audio Transcription.

Word Processing is not only an updated method of producing documents. It is more than an extension of typewriting. Nowadays many executives and administrators do their own word processing so that they can compose on to the screen and produce perfect copy in a short time.

This book has been designed to allow you (the student) to achieve the skills to be successful in RSA examinations. Before commencing a Word Processing course, it is important that you can use a QWERTY keyboard well. Learning the correct fingering methods first means that you will later be able to become a fast and accurate Word Processor operator. This book is designed for use with any Word Processing program and space has been left at relevant points for the insertion of the specific program commands. Refer to your Manufacturer's manual or your tutor for help.

Inset by 1" at both sides

You can work at your own pace at home, in a school or college, or at work. Print-out checks are provided at the back of the book so that you can be sure your work is correct before you go on to the next unit. Don't forget to use them. It is recommended that you work through the book step-by-step so that your skills and knowledge increase and develop in a logical manner.

INTRODUCTION TO WORD PROCESSING

Reset margins to 1" or 10.

View the document before printing (preview)

VIEW THE DOCUMENT
BEFORE PRINTING

As previously mentioned, in some programs, format changes such as justification and line spacing do not show on the VDU screen. You should use the view or preview function (if this is available on your progam) to check that the document format is correct before printing.

3.3 Compare the layout with the print-out check at the back of the book.

- If your layout is correct, proceed to the next step.

- If your layout is not correct, reread the instructions for formatting to get the layout right.

3.4 Save your file – use the filename **EX3A**.

3.5 Print a copy of your work.

Exercise 3B

3.6 Reformat the document you have just printed with a justified right margin.

3.7 Save your file – use the filename **EX3B**.

3.8 Print a copy of your work.

3.9 Exit the program if you have finished working or continue straight on to the next unit.

At the end of Unit 4, you will have learned how to:

a   search and replace text in a document
b   spellcheck a document
c   spellcheck a block of text.

Search and replace

In word processing, it is possible to find automatically a given word and exchange it for another given word throughout a document. An example of the way in which this function could be used is a letter being sent out from a school to parents. It would be very easy to produce some letters that referred to 'your son' and some that referred to 'your daughter', or every occurrence of 'he' could be changed to 'she'.

SEARCH AND REPLACE TEXT

Some programs allow you to confirm that replacement is required every time it finds the text to be searched for. If this function is present, it is a good idea to use it, particularly in examinations.

Exercise 4A

4.1   Retrieve the document **EX1A** from your disk and, using the search and replace function, change **book** to **publication** in the second and fourth paragraphs.

4.2   Change the format of the document as follows:

● justified right margin

● inset both margins by 5 spaces (¹/₂ inch).

4.3   View the document if possible to check the format changes.

Exercise 4B

4.4   Retrieve the document **EX2A** from your disk. Using the search and replace function, change **Word Processing** to **WP** in the third paragraph.

4.5   Change the format of the document as follows:

● justified right margin

● double-line spacing for second paragraph

● inset *left margin only* 5 spaces (¹/₂ inch).

4.6   View the document if possible to check the format changes.

Spellcheck

Most word-processing programs have a spellchecking facility. The spellcheck memory contains thousands of words, but doesn't include many proper names (e.g., cities, surnames, etc.) or some acceptable abbreviations (e.g., VDU). If you were going to use an unusual word fairly frequently that was not already in the spellcheck memory, you could actually *add* it to the list. Spellcheck would never stop on that word again.

Exercise 4C

4.7 Start a new document. Key in the following text – retain all the deliberate spelling and keying in mistakes (these have been circled) for the purpose of this exercise:

```
SALE OF RENAULT 18 SALOON CAR

With reference to your enquiry about the sale of my Renault 18
saloon car which I recieved yesterday, I can supply you with
the following details:

The registration number is C476 TWR.  The colour is Mctellic
Blue.  The engine has a 1600 cubiccapacity.

The vehical is taxed for 6 months and has a
12-month MOT certificate.  All the bodywork is in exccelent
condition.  The car has been garage maintaned and serviced
regularily from new.
```

SPELLCHECK A DOCUMENT

4.8 Move the cursor to the top of the document and run the spellcheck facility.

The word **Renault** will probably be queried – this is because the word is unlikely to be in the spellcheck dictionary although it is not necessarily spelt incorrectly. Check that you have copied the word correctly and then tell spellcheck that you wish to accept the word.

The word **recieved** should be queried – this time the word is definitely spelt wrongly. Correct the spelling (**received**) using your program spellcheck commands.

The text **C476** is queried (the letter C makes C476 a word) – again this entry is correct but not part of spellcheck's memory – accept the word.

The text **TWR** is queried – accept the word.

The text **Mctellic** is queried – this time the word is so badly spelt that spellcheck probably cannot offer any suitable replacements. Use your program's spellcheck commands to edit the word. Delete **Mctellic** and type in the correct word **Metallic.**

The text **cubiccapacity** is queried – repeat the edit procedure to go back and insert a space between the words **cubic** and **capacity** which are run together.

4.9 Continue with spellcheck, either accepting or replacing text as appropriate.

4.10 Replace the word **car** with **vehicle** in the paragraphs but not in the heading.

4.11 Save and print your document – use the filename **EX4C.**

SPELLCHECK A BLOCK OF TEXT

4.12 Exit the program if you have finished working or continue straight on to the next unit.

> **HANDY TIP** **To spellcheck a block of text:** If you don't want to check the entire document, or even a whole page, you may be able to limit the spellcheck to check a highlighted block of text. You can try this out on any future text you key in.

At the end of Unit 5, you will have learned how to:

a   embolden text, before typing and during editing
b   underline text, before typing and during editing
c   centre text, before typing and during editing.

Emphasizing text

You have already practised using CAPITALS, inset margins and used double-line spacing as methods of text emphasis. Three additional methods of emphasizing text are described below:

Bold type (double print to make it look darker) is a method of emphasizing words or phrases (especially headings) to make them more noticeable and to stress their importance to the reader.

<u>Underline</u> is used in a similar way to embolden for text emphasis.

Centred text

Centring of text, particularly headings, emphasizes the text. Main headings are often centred while subheadings are typed at the left margin.

EMBOLDEN TEXT BEFORE KEYING IN

UNDERLINE TEXT BEFORE KEYING IN

CENTRE TEXT BEFORE KEYING IN

The centring function is useful when preparing certain documents such as menus, where an attractive display is important.

In some programs, the emphasized text can be seen on screen as it will be when printed on paper. However, in other programs, codes are displayed on the screen so that the operator can see where the commands were inserted and deleted, but the text itself remains the same in appearance.

Exercise 5A

Starting a new document:

5.1   **Enter:** Appropriate commands in your program to start bold.
     Type: **This sentence is typed in bold.**
     Enter: Appropriate commands in your program to stop bold.
     Press: ↵ twice.

5.2   **Enter:** Appropriate commands in your program to start underline.
     Type: <u>This sentence is typed with underline.</u>
     Enter: Appropriate commands in your program to stop underline.
     Press: ↵ twice.

5.3   **Enter:** Appropriate commands in your program to centre text.
     Type: This sentence is centred.
     Press: ↵ twice. (Return usually cancels the centre command.)

5.4   Delete the text on your screen.

Exercise 5B

5.5   Starting a new document, practise combining methods of text emphasis by typing the following short menu. Each line should be centred, bold and/or underline being added where shown:

<u>**LYNDHURST HOTEL**</u> ← bold & underline

<u>MENU</u>

Soup of the Day
Melon & Grape Cocktail
Egg Mayonnaise

Roast Dinner of the Day
Salmon Hollandaise } bold
Courgette Bake
Chicken Kashmir

Lyndhurst Chocolate Gateau
Fresh Fruit Salad
Apple Charlotte
Selection of Local Cheeses

<u>Coffee & Mints served in Lounge Area</u>

5.6   Save and print your work – use the filename **EX5B**.

Exercise 5C

5.7   Starting a new document, key in the following exercise, using bold and underline where shown:

TEXT PROCESSING HINTS

<u>UNDERSTANDING THE DRAFT COPY</u>

HANDWRITING – make sure you can read <u>all</u> the words written in longhand. If any words are not clear, <u>look for the same</u> <u>letter formations</u> in other parts of the draft where they may be more legible. If you still have difficulty, read the document for context to try to get the sense of it.

CORRECTIONS – make yourself <u>familiar</u> with the standard correction and amendment signs.

ABBREVIATIONS – make yourself <u>familiar</u> with the standard abbreviation signs. Remember, there are some abbreviations such as etc or eg which should remain in their abbreviated form.

5.8   Save your work – use the filename **EX5C**. (There is no need to print your work at this stage.)

EMBOLDEN TEXT DURING EDITING

UNDERLINE TEXT DURING EDITING

CENTRE TEXT DURING EDITING

> **HANDY TIP** **Emphasizing text during editing:** It is possible to emphasize text which has already been keyed in. The normal procedure is to position the cursor on the first character of the text to be emphasized, 'shade' the text and then insert the appropriate commands.

15

Exercise 5D

5.9   Add more text emphasis to the document you have just keyed in:

- ● Centre the subheading 'UNDERSTANDING THE ...'

- ● Put all the circled words into bold print.

- ● Underline all the underlined words shown on the copy below.

TEXT PROCESSING HINTS

UNDERSTANDING THE DRAFT COPY

HANDWRITING - make sure you can read all the words
written in longhand. If any words are not clear, look
for the same letter formations in other parts of the
draft where they may be more legible. If you still have
difficulty, read the document for context to try to get
the sense of it.

CORRECTIONS - make yourself familiar with the standard
correction and amendment signs.

ABBREVIATIONS - make yourself familiar with the standard
abbreviation signs. Remember, there are some
abbreviations such as etc or eg which should remain in
their abbreviated form.

5.10   Save and print your work – use the filename **EX5D**.

Removing text emphasis

You may be asked to remove text emphasis, e.g., changing text from bold to ordinary type.

REMOVE TEXT EMPHASIS

In most word-processing programs, it is necessary to delete the embedded codes for the text emphasis. These codes may be visible on screen all the time or they may be hidden.

Exercise 5E

5.11   Retrieve the text you created in Exercise 5D (unless it is already on screen) and delete all the text emphasis throughout the whole document.

5.12   View the document to check that all text emphasis has been removed. (There is no need to print your work.)

5.13   Exit the program if you have finished working or continue straight on to the next unit.

At the end of Unit 6, you will have revised all the skills introduced in Units 1–5 and you will be ready to try an RSA CLAIT mock assignment.

Exercise 6A

1 Load your program and, starting a new document, key in the following text using a ragged right margin (don't forget to type your full name at the top of the document):

```
TEXT PROCESSING

In addition to editing facilities, text formatting can be
carried out.  Editing includes the insertion and deletion of
text from single characters to large paragraphs.

Formatting features include the facilities for changing the
line spacing and the margins and altering the format in which
the text is presented.

One example of changing the format is switching from a ragged
right margin to a justified right margin or vice versa.

An efficient operator would key in the text fairly quickly and
then proof-read the work and correct any errors.  At the same
time, decisions can be made about the best way of setting out
the work for maximum effect.  A text editor is very much
concerned with potential readers of the finished document and
should try to use effective presentation techniques so that
the author's intended message is transmitted as simply and
clearly as possible.
```

2 Use the spellcheck facility to check your work for spelling errors.

3 Compare your work *on screen* with the printed text above. Proofread carefully and make any necessary amendments.

4 Save and print your work – use the filename **EX6A**.

Exercise 6B

5 Retrieve **EX6A** if it is not already on screen.

6 On the first line, insert the word **text** before **editing**. In the last paragraph, insert the words **very carefully** before **proof-read**.

7 Delete the paragraph beginning **One example of** …

8 Insert the following paragraph after the second paragraph:

```
Emboldening, underlining, changing line spacing and margins
are methods of making words, sentences or paragraphs stand out
from the remainder of the text.  These draw the reader's
attention to key points.
```

9 In the paragraph beginning **In addition to** … insert **word processors also allow** following the word **facilities**,

In the second line change **can** to **to**.

10   In the paragraph beginning **Emboldening** ...., delete **These draw** and replace with **Emphasis draws**.

11   Reformat the document to:

     a   double-line spacing

     b   justified right margin

     c   inset both margins by 5 characters (¹/₂ inch).

12   Centre and underline the heading.

13   Save and print your work – use the filename **EX6B**.

14   Exit the program if you have finished working or clear your screen and continue straight on to the next exercise.

Exercise 6C

15   Starting a new document, key in the text below using an unjustified right margin:

```
MORE WORD PROCESSING TERMINOLOGY

A word processor operator talks to the computer through its
keys.

The operator gives instructions to the computer in the form
of commands.  These commands are given at the appropriate
point when text is being keyed in or being edited.  For
example, before typing an underlined heading, the operator
will insert a command to begin underlining: at the end of
the heading, another command is inserted to stop
underlining.  Because the commands are 'set into' the text,
they are called EMBEDDED COMMANDS.

Many large organisations use the MAILMERGE or MAILSHOT
capability of a word processor.  The names and addresses of
customers are stored as one file: a standard letter is
stored as another file.  The two files are merged at the
time of printing and each customer receives a letter which
appears to have been individually prepared for them.

Some people think that this facility has been over-used
recently as it has resulted in a large increase in
unsolicited 'junk mail'.
```

16   Save and print your work – use the filename **EX6C**.

Exercise 6D

17　Retrieve the file **EX6C** if it is not already on screen.

18　Insert **or CODES** after **EMBEDDED COMMANDS** at the end of the second paragraph.

19　Delete the first paragraph beginning **A word processor operator** …

20　In the paragraph beginning **The operator** …., insert the words **word processor** before **operator** in the first line.

Delete the sentence beginning **For example, before** …

21　Insert **latter** before **facility** in the last paragraph and replace **over-used** with **used far too much**.

22　Insert the following paragraph at the end of the document:

```
However, most employers and office workers would agree that
word processing is a much more effective and interesting use
of the human resource than bashing away on a manual typewriter
and re-typing the whole document each time a change is
required.
```

23　Centre the heading and put in bold.

24　Reformat the document to:

 a　justified right margin

 b　double-line spacing

 c　inset both margins by 5 characters.

25　Save and print your work – use the filename **EX6D**.

26　Exit the program.

At the end of Unit 7, you will have practised an RSA CLAIT word-processing mock assignment:

a   within approximately two hours
b   with no more than three data-entry errors
c   with no errors in system/machine manipulation.

It is not necessary to follow the line endings shown in the copy – allow the program's wordwrap facility to make line endings for you.

1   Start up your word-processing system, open a new file and key in the following text:

```
FIRST AID - RESUSCITATION

Resuscitation should be attempted even if you are unsure
whether a patient is capable of being revived.  You should
always continue until: spontaneous breathing and pulse are
restored; someone else comes along to help; a doctor takes
over; or you are exhausted.  It is easiest to carry out if
the patient is lying on the back but it should be started
immediately whatever the position the patient is in.

In order to find out whether a patient is breathing, place
your ear above the patient's mouth to see if you can feel
their breath on your face.  Also, watch for movement along
the chest and abdomen.

To give mouth-to-mouth ventilation you blow air from your
lungs into the patient's mouth or nose.  The air you
breathe out contains about 16% oxygen.  This is more than
is needed to sustain life.  When you take your mouth away,
the patient should breathe out.

You should not give mouth-to-mouth ventilation if there is
any contamination from poisoning around the patient's
mouth, if there are serious facial injuries or if there is
recurrent vomiting.
```

2   Proofread your work, correct errors, save and print a copy of the document using an unjustified right-hand margin.

3   In the first paragraph replace the words **someone else comes along to help** with **another person takes over**.

4   In the paragraph beginning **To give mouth-to-mouth ventilation** … delete the sentence **This is more than is needed to sustain life**. Insert the words **into the patient's lungs** after the words **you breathe out**.

5   Insert the following paragraph after the paragraph beginning **In order to find out** …

```
You should also be able to observe changes in the patient's
colour - when the patient is not breathing properly the
face and lip colour is blue (cyanosis).
```

6   Delete the paragraph beginning **You should not give** …

7   Centre and embolden the heading.

8   Set in the whole document by 5 characters on each side and justify the text.

9   Change the whole document to double-line spacing.

10 Save and print one copy.

11 Ensure that the document is stored on disk and close down the system.

Unfamiliar/foreign words

At the end of Unit 8, you will have learned how to:

a   reproduce unfamiliar and foreign words correctly, copying the spelling exactly as shown

b   proofread your work carefully, checking in particular the correct reproduction of unfamiliar and foreign words.

Text containing unfamiliar or foreign words

Each branch of commerce and each industry has its own vocabulary or 'jargon'.

It is vital that you take extra care when you are keying in words which are not familiar to you. If you come across a word which is new to you at work, note how it is spelt and copy it exactly, letter for letter. If you think the word is likely to crop up again, write it down in a small notebook so that next time you see it you won't need to ask for help and you are sure to get it right.

You should take special care with names of people or organizations, addresses, amounts of money, etc. It is a good idea to keep a note of regular contacts or clients.

Proofreading is particularly important with unfamiliar material. Check your work carefully yourself and, if possible, ask a colleague to check the work too. You could do the same for them!

Exercise 8A

8.1   Starting a new document, key in the following text, copying the unfamiliar words carefully:

INTERNATIONAL COMMUNICATIONS

As linguists, we are appallingly ill-equipped. After several years of secondary education the most that many of us can manage is a smattering of Franglais. On the other hand, we expect the inhabitants of our chosen holiday retreat to be able to speak perfect English and, moreover, to be able to understand our colloquialisms and regional accents.

Speaking more slowly, more loudly and with accompanying hand signs has its limitations. Such devices might go down reasonably well in Torremolinos or Aghios Nikolias but this is not the way to sell widgets in Wilhelmshaven.

Continental children are much more adventurous and innovative in their attempts to communicate in another tongue than their Anglo-Saxon counterparts.

Heads of industry and commerce in this country are urging young people to take up the challenge and to make every attempt to 'parlez Francais' and 'Deutsch sprechen' so that we are not also-rans in the free market economy.

8.2   Save and print your work – use the filename **EX8A**. Check your print-out *word for word* with the exercise above.

Exercise 8B

8.3 Starting a new document, key in the following text, copying unfamiliar words carefully:

```
CHOOSING NAMES

Some names are always popular and do not seem to have
fashionable phases.  These names are often of historical or
religious significance such as names of monarchs or saints.
James, Richard, John, Anne, Elizabeth and Jane are examples of
this type of name.  Biblical names such as Jeremiah, Malachi,
Zachariah, Bathsheba and Haggai are no longer as popular as
they were in Victorian times.

Many parents like to choose a name which is normally
associated with a particular part of the United Kingdom.  The
Irish might choose Sean, Bridget, Seamus, Caitlin or Clodagh.
The Scots might prefer Catriona, Morag, Alistair or Iain.
Welsh names sometimes cause spelling and pronunciation
problems for the rest of us - Siobhan, Rhian, Sian, Ifor and
Gwynneth are examples.
```

8.4 Save and print your work – use the filename **EX8B**. Check your print-out *word for word* with the exercise above.

8.5 Exit the program if you have finished working or continue straight on to the next unit.

At the end of Unit 9, you will have learned how to recognize:

a   some of the common text correction signs and make corresponding amendments to text.

b   abbreviations used in the RSA Core Text Processing Skills syllabus and type the abbreviated words in full without error

c   uncorrected typographical errors and make the necessary amendments to text

d   uncorrected errors of agreement and make the necessary amendments to text.

Typescript containing correction signs

A word-processor operator is seldom given work which simply requires to be copied exactly as it is. A photocopier could do the job much more quickly! Usually, the 'copy' (text which the operator copies from) contains amendments.

Examples

This sentence has been ~~changed~~. *amended*

Should be keyed in as **This sentence has been amended.**

Please delete ~~or omit~~ this word.

Should be keyed in as **Please delete this word.**

Extra words should be inserted for/ to make sense. *this sentence*

Should be keyed in as **Extra words should be inserted for this sentence to make sense.**

You may be asked to move/ words or (sentences or) phrases.

Should be keyed in as **You may be asked to move sentences or words or phrases.**

Exercise 9A

9.1   Starting a new document, key in the following text making all the necessary amendments as you go along:

CORE TEXT PROCESSING /SCHEME   *MARKING*

The work of candidates in the above examinations is assessed under three ~~main~~ headings - production rate, accuracy, *and* presentation. Each criterion must be satisfied for a pass or a distinction to be ~~given~~/ *awarded*

Production rate is the ability to ~~finish~~ the /8 tasks within the one/ allowed. *hour*   *Complete   three*

Accuracy is the ability to produce work/ error-free. A word missing or a word which is superfluous ~~also~~ counts as one error.   *which is*

Presentation refers to the ~~layout~~ of the document, eg use of (line spacing,) paper size, clean/ copy. *appearance   and uncreased*

9.2 Press return 7 times to leave a space one inch deep before starting the next exercise.

Typescript containing abbreviations

Text authors often use abbreviations when writing out copy which is to be processed by a word-processor operator. In the work situation, you would quickly get used to individual authors' 'shorthand'.

The following list shows the abbreviations you can expect to come across in the Core Text Processing Skills examination:

accom.	accommodation	recom.	recommend
advert(s).	advertisement(s)	ref(s).	reference(s)
bel.	believe	resp.	responsible
bus.	business	sec(s).	secretary/ies
co(s).	company/ies	sep.	separate
def.	definitely	thro'	through
necy.	necessary	sh.	shall
opp(s).	opportunity/ies	wh.	which
rec.	receive	w.	with
recd.	received		

Note: The full stop is used after the abbreviation to show that it is shortened. You should not type the full stop (unless the word is at the end of a sentence, of course).

You will also be expected to key in the following in full:

- days of the week, e.g., Wednesday, Thursday

- months of the year, e.g., February, September

- words in addresses, e.g., Grove, Drive, Crescent

- complimentary closes, e.g., Yours faithfully/sincerely.

You *may not* take the above list with you into the examination–so you need to learn them. However, you may use your spellcheck facility and, of course, you may use a dictionary.

Exercise 9B

9.3 Key in the following text typing all the abbreviations in full as you go along:

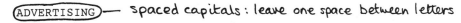

(ADVERTISING)— spaced capitals: leave one space between letters

```
We do not realise how much we are affected by adverts. in our
everyday lives.  Large cos. employ specialists from a sep.
firm to advise and prepare their campaigns.  An advertising
agency will recom. the best type of advert. and, if required,
will be resp. for the whole process right thro' to
presentation of the finished video, film, display, or
newspaper page.

A bus. wh. is just being set up will def. find it necy. to
advertise its products or services widely if it is to be a
success.  There are many inexpensive methods wh. give a small
bus. the opp. to publicise itself - for example, printed paper
bags, posters or handbills.
```

9.4 Save and print your work – use the filename **EX9B**.

Typescript containing typographical errors

Text processing may involve putting right any mistakes made in previous print-outs. Watch out for uncorrected spelling errors and transposition errors.

Examples

This sentance contains 3 <u>speling errers</u>.

should be keyed in as:

This **sentence** contains 3 **<u>spelling errors</u>**.

This sentence contians 2 <u>transpositoin errors</u>.

should be keyed in as:

This sentence **contains** 2 **<u>transposition</u>** <u>errors</u>.

In the RSA Core Text Processing Skills examination, any words which are incorrect will be circled. It is up to you to decide what is wrong and to key in the word correctly.

Exercise 9C

9.5 Starting a new document, key in the following text correcting all the words which are circled as you go along:

PROOFREADING YOUR WORK — *spaced caps: leave 3 spaces between words, one space between letters*

In text processing examinatoins, candidates are often expected to be able to find any errers wh. appear in the copy and to make surethat all these errors have been corected in their final typewriten or printed work.

At elementary and intermediate levells, any such errors aer circled and the typist simply has to identify what is wrong and put it rihgt.

It is very importent to cheque all your work before you take it out of your typewriter, or before you print our if you are using a word processer.

Remember your word-processing program probably has a spellcheck facility which allows you to check your work for spelling errors before printing. Why not use it now?

9.6 Press return 7 times to leave a space one inch deep before starting the next exercise.

Typescript containing errors of agreement

As you are keying in text, you should make sure that what you are typing makes sense. You should watch out for errors of agreement when the noun and the verb in a sentence do not agree.

Examples

This class of girls are irritating.

This should be keyed in as **This class of girls is irritating** (because there is only *one* class). If there were more than one class, you would key in: **These classes of girls are irritating**.

The difference between the two word-processing programs were demonstrated by the supervisor.

This should be keyed in as **The difference between the two word-processing programs was demonstrated by the supervisor** (because there are *two* programs but only *one* difference).

Exercise 9D

9.7   Key in the following text correcting the circled words as you go along:

METHODS OF ENHANCING TEXT ← embolden heading

The most commonly used (method) are bold and underline.

The Core Text Processing Skills examination may be taken on a typewriter or a word processor. Your typewriter could be a manual (ones) an electric one or an electronic one. Manual and electric typewriters (is) not usually able to produce emboldened text so the main method of emphasis (are) underlining.

Word processors also (allows) the 'font' to be changed so that the characters (varies) in size and appearance. Sophisticated programs wh. are often expensive to buy, (offers) a wide choice of typestyle.

9.8   Save and print your work – use the filename **EX9D**.

Exercise 9E

9.9 Starting a new document, key in the following text (in double-line spacing with a ragged right margin). Correct all the circled errors as you go along, and make amendments as shown. Retain all the abbreviations underlined with〰〰 :

ABBREVIATIONS ← *underline heading*

Core (Test) Processing Skills (examinatoins) contain abbreviations which have (tobe) reproduced ᵢₙ/ full and correctly (spellt). The days of the (weak) should always be typed in full and with a ~~big~~ capital (leter) at the (begining), eg T̲h̲u̲r̲s̲. should be Thursday, W̲e̲d̲. should be (Wenesday).

expanded
In addition, the (mouths) of the year should be ~~represented in full~~ eg J̲a̲n̲. should be (Janury), F̲e̲b̲. should be (Febuary), O̲c̲t̲. should be (OCTober).

In addresses, (Cressent), Drive, (AVenue), Grove should be typed in full.   Other examples are Road for R̲d̲., (Streeet) for S̲t̲.

Many students make mistakes when typing the complimentary close at the (edn) of a letter.   Yours always has a (cpaital) letter but sincerely, (faithfuly) and (truely) begin with a small letter.

Abbreviations are ∨written (always) with a full stop after them. This is to be (ommitted), of (coarse), when typed in full.

9.10 Save and print your work – use the filename **EX9E**.

9.11 Exit the program if you have finished working or continue straight on to the next unit.

At the end of Unit 10, you will have practised keying in text from copy which is handwritten and contains amendments and corrections.

Typing from manuscript copy

'Manuscript' means written by hand. Word-processor operators are often given work in handwritten form.

When typing from the handwritten draft, make sure you can read *all* the words written in longhand. If any words are not clear, *look for the same letter formations* in other parts of the draft where they may be more legible. If you still have difficulty, read the document for context to try to get the sense of it.

The standard correction signs and abbreviations which you learned in the previous unit will appear in manuscript copy as well as in typescript.

Exercise 10A

10.1 Key in the following text, using a ragged right margin:

Following Manuscript Copy ← CAPS

When you have to type from a page of manuscript copy, first read it thro' carefully. Clarify any words, figures and abbreviations wh. are not immed. clear by looking elsewhere in the draft for the same letter formations. Reading the draft for meaning will also help you to interpret any illegible words.

Pay careful attention to editing – look out for text wh. has been crossed out and therefore should not be keyed in & also for text wh. needs to be inserted at /points. /marked It can sometimes be/ to mistakes a comma ^for a full stop.   easy

Because handwriting takes up more room than typescript you will have to judge ~~the amount of space the draft will occupy~~, set suitable margins + make your own line-endings (or allow wordwrap to do so).

(the finished layout of the draft)

10.2 Press return 7 times to leave one inch before the next exercise.

Some additional text corrections signs

You have already learnt basic correction signs in Unit 9. Look at the following examples of other signs which you may see on typewritten or manuscript text.

⌐ or //

Start a new paragraph where you see either of these signs. The words NP (new paragraph) may also appear in the margin.

The 'run on' sign is used when two paragraphs should be joined together.

To join two paragraphs, put the cursor on the first character of the second paragraph and press ⟵ Del twice.

If you see a tick inside a circle in the margin, look for a word (or words) in the text which has a dotted line underneath it. These two signs mean that you should insert the word with the dotted line underneath, even though it may have been crossed out.

⟨✓⟩ When you type this sentence, ~~insert~~ this word.

should be typed as **When you type this sentence, insert this word.**

word 1 word 2 This sign means that you should type word 2 before word 1. This is called transposition.

Two words in sentence this are the wrong way round.

should be typed as **Two words in this sentence are the wrong way round.**

You may also have to transpose words vertically, for example if they are in a list.

	should be typed as:	
Dot Matrix		Dot Matrix
Laser		Ink Jet
Ink Jet		Laser
Thermal		Thermal

Exercise 10B

10.3 Key in the following text, using a ragged right margin:

Language Skills in Text Processing ← heading in caps

A good knowledge of English is very important because the copy wh. are given to the word processor will operator not be 'perfect'. It may be in any of the formats: following

typescript
manuscript
dictated & written in shorthand
dictated onto audio-tape.

More often than not, it will be necy. for the operator to make amendments & corrections to the original draft. Some of the corrections and amendments will be clearly identified marked ✓ but others may be questionable, and this is where the operator's language skills becomes vital. A wide vocabulary & knowledge of the subject matter will be of great assistance & an understanding of grammar & punctuation will help the operator, and eventually the reader, to understand interpret the writer's message correctly. You should develop your language skills by reading a wide variety of materials and by learning about the bus. or industry in wh. you are involved.

If you are learning word processing as a student, you will also be acquiring a business-based vocabulary thro' the text wh. you work w. and the other subjects in your programme. ✓
course

10.4 Save and print a copy of your work – use the filename **EX10**.

10.5 Exit the program if you have finished working or continue straight on to the next unit.

Personal business letters

At the end of Unit 11 you will have learned how to:

a   complete a personal business letter
b   insert a new page marker
c   complete an envelope.

In the Core Text examination, you will be expected to type a personal business letter from manuscript on plain A4 paper. This will include some abbreviations, amendments and correction signs.

Keying in a personal business letter

● Type your own address (or sender's address) at top left-hand side of the letter.

● Block everything at the left-hand margin (date, addressee, salutation, subject heading, all paragraphs and complimentary close) – do not indent paragraphs or centre items.

● Always remember to date the letter with today's date at the left margin – it is also acceptable to position the date flush with the right margin.

● Use open punctuation – no punctuation above or below the body of the letter (i.e., date, addressee, salutation or complimentary close).

● Leave at least one clear line space between the different parts of the letter – date, addresses, salutation, etc.

● Leave at least one clear line space between paragraphs.

● If the salutation is formal, e.g., 'Dear Sir or Madam', finish your letter with the complimentary close: 'Yours faithfully'.

● If the salutation is informal, e.g., 'Dear Mrs Smith', finish your letter with the complimentary close: 'Yours sincerely'.

● Leave several clear lines for the person sending the letter to write their signature.

Exercise 11A

11.1 Key in the exercise on the following page. Follow the layout of the letter as shown but allow wordwrap to make the line endings. There is no need for you to type the instructions in the margin – they are simply a guide to help you identify the different parts of a letter.

11.2 Save your work – use the filename **EX11A**.

```
        Secretarial Department                          address
        Greenborough College                                of
        Plummet Street                                   sender
        GREENBOROUGH
        GR1 3UZ
Turn up 2
        Today's Date                               date in full
Turn up 2
        Mr/Miss Student                       name and address
        22 Somewhere Street                                 of
        ANYTOWN                                      addressee
        AN1 6HA

Turn up 2
        Dear Mr/Miss Student                         salutation
Turn up 2
        This is an example of a personal letter.  There is no
        punctuation in the addresses or the date, and no comma
        after the salutation.  Punctuation is used only in the
        body of the letter when it is necessary.  In the fully
        blocked style, every line begins at the left margin.
Turn up 2                                          body of letter
        You will be asked to type a personal letter and envelope
        in the RSA Core Text Processing Skills Examination.
        Study the layout of this letter and set your letter out
        in this way in the examination.
Turn up 2
        Yours sincerely                            complimentary
Turn up 6                                                  close

                                              space for signature


        A S Lavedriver (Mrs)                   name of signatory
                                                        (sender)
```

Envelopes

In Task 2 of the Core Text Processing Skills examination, you will be asked to produce an envelope to go with the letter. The envelope you are given is DL size (about the size of a sheet of A4 folded into three). The flap of the envelope should be at the right or the bottom depending on its style. You may have to produce your envelopes on a typewriter – this is perfectly acceptable.

Begin approximately *one-third across* and *half-way down* the envelope.

Key in each part of the address on a separate line.

Key in the postcode on a *separate line*, leaving one space between the two parts of the postcode.

Key in the town in CAPITALS.

```
┌────────────────────────────────────────┐
│                                        │
│                                        │
│         Mr/Miss Student                │
│         22 Somewhere Street            │
│         ANYTOWN                        │
│         AN1 6HA                        │
│                                        │
│                                        │
└────────────────────────────────────────┘
```

11.3 Produce an envelope for the letter you completed in Exercise 11A by following the guidelines given above.

11.4 Unless it is already on your screen, retrieve the document **EX11A**.

NEW PAGE MARKER

11.5 Position the cursor at the end of the document. Insert a new page marker.

Exercise 11B

11.6 Key in the following document from the manuscript draft:

74 Richmond Rd.
Wellerton Park
BRADFORD
BD19 2JS

Mr A Sykes
Home Decorating Services Ltd
21-23 Alton St.
LEEDS
LS1 2BY

Dear Mr Sykes

With ref. to your recent advert. in the Daily News, *(an estimate)*
would you please arrange to call at my address
✓ let me have ~~a price~~ for decorating ✗ 3
bedrooms and a kitchen.

I wd. be grateful if you could bring w. you
any colour ~~charts~~ charts, wallpaper samples & paint
ranges etc. wh. ~~might~~ could be of interest to me and ✓
wh. you would recom.

I sh. be glad if you will confirm that your bus. *(sometime)*
is def. reliable and that you wd. be able to carry
out the work in Feb. when I sh. be on holiday
and my accom. will be empty.

You can contact me thro' my sec. at my co. / on *(~~works~~ office)*
telephone no. 93-653168 anytime ~~between~~ during
working hours.

Yours scly.

M Davies (Miss)

11.7 Save and print your work – use the filename **EX11B**. Keep your print-out of the first letter (**EX11A**) for future reference on correct letter layout.

11.8 Produce an envelope to go with the letter in Exercise 11B.

11.9 Exit the program if you have finished working or continue straight on to the next unit.

Task 1

Key in the following document using a ragged right margin. Remember to enter today's date. Save and print a copy of your file – use the filename **CON21**.

26 Luster Ave.

SHEFFIELD

SH2 3 GS

Mr S Swallow
26 Foster St.
LOOE
Cornwall
LO5 BR2

Dr. Mr Swallow

Thank you for yr. letter, along w. brochure ~ price list of garden equipment, ⌐seeds, bulbs⌐ and shrubs wh. I recd. last week.

I am def. interested in your range of pergolas and garden furniture which I bel. you have on special offer ~~to~~ until the end of the yr. [As I am part of a large gardening society I would be interested to know if you could ~~offer~~ any discounts for bulk ~~mass~~ orders ~ the ~~soft~~ quantities ~~you would require~~ it would be necy. to order before discount was available.

I am also anxious to purchase a shrub entitled 'Kalmia ~~&~~ Latiofolia' which is not shown in your current ~~current~~ brochure ~ wonder if you can ~~possibly~~ recom. another supplier of this item.

yours scly.

R Thomas (Miss)

Task 2

Produce an envelope to go with the letter in task 1.

Task 3

Key in the following document using single-line spacing and a justified right margin. Make amendments as shown and correct the circled words. Save and print a copy of your file – use the filename **CON22**:

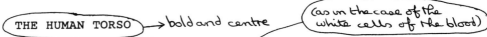

THE HUMAN TORSO → bold and centre   (as in the case of the white cells of the blood)

The human torso ~~are~~ is made up of / millions and millions of cells which sometimes ~~workes~~ single, but more often, when they are concerned in carrying out the same ~~sort~~ kind of function, are grouped together in what ~~were~~ are called organs such as the heart, kidneys, liver & so on.

The skeleton, w. the (mussels) attached to its (seperate) bones and covered by the skin and (it's) appendages, gives the torso its characteristic ~~look~~ / and supports the structure. appearance
(whole)

Inside ~~both~~ the (backbone) and (skull), or spine, and protected by them are the brain and spinal cord. (Connecting these parts, are the nerves. There is a very close connection between the nervous system and the muscles, and because life is largely (manetained) by movements of ~~many different~~ kinds these two (were) often spoken of as the master tissues of the torso.
and making possible communications between them and the rest of the body

Task 4

Retrieve the document **CON22**. Amend the document as follows:

Search for the word **torso** and replace throughout with **body**.

Change the heading to spaced capitals and copy to the end of the document (retain the centred display).

Change the right margin to ragged.

Insert the following text so that is becomes the second paragraph – for this paragraph only, use double-line spacing and inset by 1 inch at left and right margins.

Save and print a copy of your file – use the filename **CON23**.

When (tow) or more organs are grouped together to serve some (special) function, such ~~as~~ a group is spoken of as a system; we have, ~~have~~, for example, the circulatory, the respiratory, the digestive and the reproductive systems.

Task 1

Key in the following document. Save and print a copy of your file – use the filename **CORE1**:

14 Fairview Rd.
BOLTON
BT4 5RM

Mr B West
Betterbuy Products
23 Park St.
KEIGHLEY
KH9 2AP

Dr. Mr West

Thank you for sending your brochure + price list of novelties and fancy goods.

I am sec. of the local Friends of Nature Society and we are interested in purchasing some of yr. goods for our fund-raising campaign.

We wd. like to know if it would be possible to have our Society logo engraved on some of your goods. It is a beaver in a circle w. the words "Friends of Nature" going round the outer edge.

We would be particularly interested in the range of tailor-made sweatshirts you have on offer, providing the logo could def. be printed on these garments.

I look forward to your reply.

Yours scly.

V Lambert (Mrs)

Task 2

Produce an envelope to go with the letter in task 1.

Task 3

Key in the following document using single-line spacing. Make amendments as shown and correct the circled words. Save and print a copy of your file – use the filename **CORE3**:

```
NATURE'S ARCHITECTS

                    wide
Animals use a variety of materials in building (thier) homes.

The structures (is) often complex, ingenious and sometimes

enormous in scale.


As its name implies, the paper wasp uses a paper-like material

by chewing wood.  (which it produces itself)


Weaver ants 'sew' leaves together. After the thread has been

silk-spun by the ant larva, it is passed backwards and
        forth
forwards from one leaf to another, gripped between the jaws of

an adult ant.


Honey bees make (there) combs from wax that is formed in flakes

(flakes) underneath the worker bees' abdomens. (this) honeycombed

pattern of the wasps nest is strong, yet light, and has been

copied in the design of some aircraft wings.


Termite towers are made from mud (mixes) with the saliva of

termites - a (micxture) which sets hard as concrete.
```

At the end of Unit 14 you will have learnt how to:

a set a new tab
b delete an individual tab setting
c change the position of a tab setting
d delete all tab settings together
e reset tabs at regular settings.

Tabulation

Presenting data in columns is often used within letters, memos and reports to convey information quickly and clearly. Tabulated columns of information are also used for separate tables and accounts.

Use capitals or underlining to emphasize the column headings and leave a clear line space between the heading and the information below.

Leave sufficient space between the headings to allow for the longest line of each column.

Count the longest line in each of the columns and set tab stops in the appropriate places. It looks better if you leave equal amounts of space between columns (e.g., three spaces) but this is not absolutely necessary.

Key in the columns in double- or single-line spacing according to the instructions provided or amount of space available on the page.

Where numbers are included in the column work you may choose to use a left-aligned tab (to block them to the left), or a right-aligned tab (to block them to the right) or a decimal tab (to wrap them around the decimal point):

For example:	72	72	72.10
	6	6	6.00
	104	104	104.00
	left-aligned tab	right-aligned tab	decimal tab

You should leave one clear line after the tabulation work before continuing with any further portions of text.

On some keyboards the tab key is labelled **Tab** and on others shown as

On some word-processing programs the tab settings are defaulted (i.e., previously set) to every **5 spaces** (or **1/2 inch**). Each time you press the tab key you indent the line by 5 spaces (1/2 inch).

If you press the tab key while in typeover mode, you simply move the cursor along the line 5 spaces at a time without indenting the text.

There will be times, especially if you are typing a table with uneven columns, when you will need to *set*, *delete* or *change* the position of the default tab settings.

TABULATION – SET NEW TAB

TABULATION – DELETE INDIVIDUAL TAB SETTING

TABULATION – CHANGE THE POSITION OF TAB SETTING

TABULATION – DELETE ALL TAB SETTINGS TOGETHER

TABULATION – RESET TABS AT REGULAR SETTINGS

Exercise 14A

14.1 Set tabs to every 5 spaces if these are not already set by the program default.

Key in the following text – after typing the bracketed letter at the beginning of each line press the tab key once to reach the first set tab stop:

```
HOLIDAY INN

A)    SITUATION:  5 miles south of London
B)    CONDITION:  Well-maintained and modernised.
C)    ACCOMMODATION:  See details on attached sheet.
D)    PRICE:  On application.
```

14.2 Clear your screen (you do not need to save your work at this stage).

Exercise 14B

14.3 Key in the following exercise (press the tab key before each numerical entry of the table):

```
EASYCLEAN SALES - JULY

HALIFAX    145  125  176  110  145  126
LEEDS      105  158  169  145  128  177
DEWSBURY   180  140  150  145  126  110
```

14.4 Press ⏎ several times to leave a gap before the next exercise.

Exercise 14C

14.5 Delete all existing tabs. Then, set left-aligned tab stops at **21** and **58** only – *refer to the glossary instructions for setting, deleting and changing tabs.*

14.6 Check that you have set the tab stops in the correct position by pressing the tab key twice. The cursor should move across the screen to position **21** and then **58** on your ruler line (there should be a status indicator on your screen to give the current position of the cursor).

14.7 Key in the following:

```
STOCK NO    DESCRIPTION                        SALE PRICE (£)

DEV356      Green corduroy pleated skirt       12.99
TYR359      Blue denim shirt                   17.99
CRT47       Yellow double-breasted silk blouse 26.99
ZXW35       Brown sweatshirt top               14.99
```

14.8 Press ⏎ several times to leave a gap before the next exercise.

Allocate vertical space

In single-line spacing: 6 clear lines = 1 inch.

(Remember to turn up an extra line space to leave a given measurement clear.)

Blocked capitals

Press: Caps lock key

Centre text

To centre text before keying in:

To centre text already keyed in:

To remove centring:

Change logged disk drive to A

Clear the screen

Copy a block of text

Create a new document

Cursor movement

Move cursor to required position   Use the arrow keys (cursor keys) ⟶ ⟵ ⇕
to move cursor to required position.

Move to top of document

Move to end of document

Move left word by word

Move right word by word

Move to end of line

Move to start of line

Delete a character

Move cursor to incorrect character.
Press: Del   *or*

Move cursor to right of incorrect character.
Press: ⟵ (Del)

Delete a word

Delete a block of text

Edit text – delete and insert

Delete character(s)	Move cursor to incorrect character. **Press:** Del (delete key) *or*
	Move cursor to right of incorrect character. **Press:** ⟵ (Del)
Delete a word	
Replace text by 'overtyping' (typeover)	Move cursor to incorrect entry. **Press:** Ins key (typeover on) Overtype with correct entry. **Press:** Ins key (typeover off)
Insert characters or words	Position cursor where missing characters should be inserted: Key in the missing character(s) or word(s) Existing text will 'move over' to make room for the new text.

Embolden text

To embolden text before
keying in:

To embolden text already
keyed in:

To remove bold:

Exit the program

Help function

Indent function

To indent at left margin:

To indent at left and
right margin:

Insert text

Simply key in the missing character(s) at the
appropriate place – the existing text will
'move over' to make room for the new text.

Justified right margin

Key in text

Line length – to change to fixed length

You can fit 82 characters across A4 paper using 10 pitch. If the left and right margins are set to 1 inch, then there are 62 characters across the typing line.

To reduce this to a 'fixed' length:

(1) add all the required characters to left margin
(2) add all the required characters to right margin
(3) add some of required characters to left margin and some to right.

Line spacing

Margins (to change)

Move block of text

New page marker

Paragraphs – splitting/joining

Make a new paragraph (i.e. split an existing paragraph into two)	Move cursor to first letter of new paragraph. **Press:** ←┘ twice
Join two consecutive paragraphs into one	Move cursor to first character of second paragraph. **Press:** ←— Del twice (backspace delete key) **Press:** Spacebar (to insert space(s)) after full stop

Pitch (to change)

Print out hard copy

Check that the printer is switched on, is 'on-line' and has paper in it.

Ragged right margin

Remove text emphasis

Replace text – typeover

Move cursor to incorrect entry. **Press**: Ins key (typeover on). Overtype with correct entry. **Press** Ins key (typeover off).

Restore deleted text

Retrieve a file from disk

Save work to disk

Search and replace text

Shade a block of text

Spaced capitals

> **Press:** Caps lock key
> Leave one space after each letter.
> Leave three spaces after each word.

Spellcheck document/block of text

Switch on and load WP program

Tabulation

Set new tab:

Left-aligned tab:

Right-aligned tab:

Decimal tab:

Delete individual tab setting:

Change the position of tab setting:

Delete all tab settings together:

Reset tabs at regular settings:

Underline text

To underline text before keying in:

To underline text already keyed in:

To remove underline:

View document

View file directory

Exercise 14D

14.9 Count the longest line in each column and set tab stops in the appropriate places. (It looks better if you leave equal amounts of space between the columns, e.g., three spaces but this is not absolutely necessary.)
Key in the following:

```
JOB VACANCIES

Job No          Department          Job Description

58              Main Reception      Receptionist/Telephonist
59              Accounts            Junior Clerk
60              Marketing           Shorthand-Typist
```

14.10 Save and print a copy of your work (Exercises 14B, 14C, and 14D). Use the filename **EX14**.

14.11 Reset the tab stops to every 5 spaces.

14.12 Exit the program if you have finished working or continue straight on to the next unit.

At the end of Unit 15 you will have learned how to recognize and expand abbreviations listed for RSA I.

This list contains *additional* RSA I abbreviations which you will need to learn and remember.

RSA I abbreviations

accom.	accommodation	rec(s).	receipt(s)
a/c(s).	account(s)	rec.	receive
ack.	acknowledge	recd.	received
advert(s).	advertisement(s)	recom.	recommend
appt(s).	appointment(s)	ref(s).	reference(s)
approx.	approximately	refd.	referred
bel.	believe	resp.	responsible
bus.	business	sec(s).	secretary/ies
cat(s).	catalogue(s)	sep.	separate
cttee(s).	committee(s)	sig(s).	signature(s)
co(s).	company/ies	suff.	sufficient
def.	definitely	temp.	temporary
dev.	develop	thro'	through
ex.	exercise		
exp(s).	expense(s)		
exp.	experience	sh.	shall
gov(s).	governments	shd.	should
gntee(s).	guarantee(s)	wh.	which
immed.	immediately	wd.	would
incon.	inconvenient/ence	w.	with
mfr(s).	manufacturer(s)	wl.	will
misc.	miscellaneous	yr(s).	years
necy.	necessary	yr(s).	yours
opp(s).	opportunity/ies	dr.	dear

Days of the week

Mon.	Monday
Tues.	Tuesday
Wed.	Wednesday

Months of the year

Jan.	January
Feb.	February
Mar.	March

Words in address

Cres.	Crescent
Dr.	Drive
Rd.	Road

Complimentary close

ffly.	faithfully
scly.	sincerely

Note: You should retain other commonly used abbreviations such as: **etc. eg. NB, Ltd** (you can retain the **&** sign in company names but you should never use the **&** sign in text).

Exercise 15A

15.1 Key in the following, expanding all the abbreviations as you go along and making any other amendments indicated. (Check that you have keyed in the correct abbreviations from the RSA I list.)

NOTICE TO STAFF

We have recd. an overwhelming response to the advert.
put up on the Staff Notice Board about the
Xmas dinner. [It will be necy. for all staff who
put ~~their~~ name on the list to ~~make~~ complete a sep.
payment voucher to cover all exps. of the dinner.
The payment wl. then be deducted from yr. wage.
A signed rec. wl. be available thro' the co. sec.
together w. the Dinner Ticket. (straight)

In order to give the cttee. suff. opp. to make
all the necy. arrangements (and since past exp.
shows that places become booked very quickly) we
wd. recom. that those staff who def. wish to
reserve a place complete a payment voucher
immed. ~~as soon as possible.~~

No places can be booked after the end of Oct.

SOCIAL CLUB CTTEE.

15.2 Exit the program if you have finished working or continue straight on to the next unit (you do not need to save or print your work at this stage).

At the end of Unit 16 you will have learned how to:

a   indent blocks of text or paragraphs (e.g., enumerated paragraphs)
b   change the line length for the whole document.

Indent – 'wrap around' or temporary indent feature

In Unit 3 you practised changing the left and right margins to inset the text to a different line length. Another method of indenting blocks of text, or paragraphs, is to use the indent function which is available on most word-processing programs.

When you press the appropriate indent key(s), the cursor moves to the first preset tab stop (usually defaulted to five spaces in from the left margin – on some word-processing programs you may have to set an indent tab yourself). As you carry on keying in, the text will 'wrap around' the indent point until you press the return key – the cursor will then go back to the original left margin.

Some word-processing programs allow you to indent the text from both the left and right margin. If the program you are using only allows you to use the indent function at the left, you would have to alter the right margin setting to indent text at the right.

> It is often more convenient to use the indent function to indent a single paragraph as shown in this example.

The indent feature is often used for displaying enumerated paragraphs as shown in Exercise 16A. If you are asked to leave a specified amount of horizontal space at any point in a task, you may choose to use either the indent function or alter the margin settings as appropriate.

INDENT FUNCTION

Exercise 16A

16.1 Key in the following exercise – remember to leave one clear line space between enumerated items. Use the indent function after typing each number to indent the paragraphs around the indent point as shown:

```
INTRODUCING COMPUTERS

1   ELECTRONIC:  The machine uses thousands of microscopic
    electronic components which can fit on to a single
    silicon microchip (smaller than the size of a finger
    nail).

2   PROGRAMMABLE:  Once an instruction is given the
    machine will carry out the task by itself - without
    the instruction it is unable to operate.

3   INFORMATION PROCESSORS:  Information is input into the
    computer (by people or machines) then processed in the
    computer and then output by the computer (by people or
    machines).
```

16.2 Press ⏎ several times to leave a gap before the next exercise.

Exercise 16B

16.3 Retrieve the file you saved from Unit 5: **EX5D**.

16.4 Using the indent function:

- Indent the document by 1 inch at left and right margins (you will need to repeat the instruction at the beginning of each paragraph as the indent code will have been cancelled by the hard return you keyed in at the end of each paragraph).

- Indent second paragraph only by a further ½ inch at left margin.

16.5 Save and print your work – use the filename **EX16B**.

Changing the line length to a fixed number of characters

You may be asked to change the 'line length' (or typing line) of a document to a fixed number of characters. This is achieved by either *indenting* (using the indent function) or *insetting* the margins. (It is not always possible in word processing to be completely accurate in this respect and examiners should be aware of this and be lenient in their marking of this feature.)

The width of A4 paper is approximately 8.2 inches (or 82 characters in 10 pitch). The 'default' margins in most word-processing programs are set at 1 inch (or 10 characters in 10 pitch) at both left and right sides. Therefore, there are normally 62 characters across the typing line. However, programs do vary so you must check the settings of the program you are using.

The extra characters to be added to the margin settings in order to reduce the typing line to a 'fixed' length can be incorporated in any of the following three ways:

a   all the required extra characters added to the left margin; or

b   all the required extra characters added to the right margin; or

c   some of the extra characters added to the left margin and some to the right (these amounts do not have to be equal).

Example

To change the line length (normally 62 characters long) to 50 characters, you could change the margin settings by adding 12 characters to the left or right margin, or add 6 characters to both.

Exercise 16C

16.6 Retrieve the file you saved from Unit 4: **EX4C**:

- Change the line length to 54 characters.

- Indent the last paragraph only by a further 1 inch at left margin.

16.7 Save and print a copy of your work – use the filename **EX16C**.

16.8 Exit the program if you have finished working or continue straight on to the next unit.

At the end of Unit 17 you will have learned how to:

a   leave specified areas of vertical space within a document
b   confirm facts by checking details from information given previously.

Allocating vertical space

It is often necessary to insert diagrams, photographs or maps on to a page which also contains text. For example, a student record card may need to have a blank space where the student's photograph could be fixed.

There are 6 lines (in single spacing) to 1 inch (the same applies to typewriters). Be sure to turn up an extra line space in order to leave the given measurement clear: if in doubt, leave a little extra space rather than less.

Examples

To leave **6** clear lines (1 inch): **press** the return key **7** times.

To leave **12** clear lines (2 inches): **press** the return key **13** times.

Confirming facts

When people are writing manuscript copy, they often leave it to the operator to fill in repeated text such as names, titles, addresses, etc. You will need to check previous correspondence and use your common sense to fill in the missing information.

In the RSA I examination you will not have to 'invent' any missing information, but you will be expected to complete the gap from information given elsewhere in the examination paper. The first letter of each missing word will be given to assist you.

Example

Mrs R Jamieson
22 Stones Drive
LEEDS

Dear Mrs J—————

With reference to your planning application for home improvements to 22 S————— D————, I must inform

(The missing words would be: Jamieson and Stones Drive.)

Exercise 17A

17.1 Use single-line spacing, justified right margin and press the return key the required number of times to leave space where shown:

```
THE FIRS   WOODLANDS AVENUE
```

```
The Firs is an imposing Victorian house set in attractive,
mature gardens of approx. 1 acre.
```
run on

Inset 12 spaces at left

```
It was built in 1857 for Jonas Appleyard, a local mill owner,
to house his large family and its servants. //The property has
spectacular, panoramic views to the south over the valley.
```
— leave 2" here for photo
```
The accom. briefly comprises on the ground floor:  entrance
hall, 3 reception rooms, large kitchen, scullery, pantry and
lavatory.
The accom. on the first floor comprises:
4 double bedrooms, 1 with en-suite bath/shower room, 1 box
room, + a large family bathroom.
```
— leave 1½" here for garden details
```
There are extensive cellars as is usual in houses of this age
+ type.  To the south-west of the house, with access from the
dining room, is an attractive hexagonal conservatory of timber
construction w. feature leaded lights. //For further details,
please contact our Halifax office.
```

*Indent last para by ½" at left
and right margins*

17.2 Save and print your work – use the filename **EX17A**.

Exercise 17B

17.3 Starting with a clear screen, key in the following text, using single-line spacing, and ragged right margin:

```
DISK OPERATING SYSTEM
```

```
DOS is the abbreviated name for Disk Operating System.  The
system allows many functions to be carried out:
```

please leave 2" here for full list

Indent ½" at both margins
```
It is poss. to see a list of all the files on a disk (the
directory).  Files may be deleted from this directory by using
a simple command at the C or A prompt.
```

```
Disks are copied and formatted through DOS.  Formatting makes
a disk ready to accept data.  It is poss. to copy a file from
one disk to another, or copy the whole contents of a disk.
```

please leave 2½" here for example

```
The directory (example above) can be printed out on paper the
this can be kept in the disk envelope as a quick ref. to the
disk's contents.
```

*The D— O— S— is used to make back-up copies
of files and disks. These shd. be kept in a
safe place and regularly up-dated.*

17.4 Save and print your work – use the filename **EX17B**.

17.5 Exit the program if you have finished or go straight on to the next unit.

At the end of Unit 18 you will have learned how to:

a   recognize the difference between a 'personal business letter'
     and a 'business letter'
b   complete a business letter
c   position special marks and enclosure marks.

In Unit 11 you learned how to produce a personal business letter on plain
A4 paper. In the RSA I examination, you will be expected to produce a
business letter on plain A4 paper. There is no need to prepare an envelope
or label in the Stage I examination.

Business letter layout

A personal business letter is the type of formal letter you might write at home to an
organization or firm referring to matters which are not connected with your work.

A business letter is written on behalf of an organization and is printed or typed
on the organization's own letterhead. This saves time and an attractive letterhead
gives a good impression of the organization. Only the name and address of the
addressee (recipient) of the letter have to be typed because the sender's details are
already printed on the letterhead.

In the RSA Stage I Word Processing examination, the business letter is to be
printed, after the examination, on plain paper. Letterheaded paper is not used at
this stage because of the difficulties there may be in feeding single sheets of the
paper into certain printers.

Refer back to Unit 11 to refresh your memory on letter layout.

Special marks and enclosure marks

Special marks are designed to draw special attention on documents and
envelopes for instructions such as:
CONFIDENTIAL, PRIVATE, PERSONAL, URGENT, FOR THE ATTENTION
OF …, etc. They should, therefore, be given some form of emphasis such as bold,
underlining or capitalization.

The special mark should be placed at the top of a document with one clear line
space above and below it.

If a letter includes a special mark this should also be included on the envelope.

Enclosure marks (Enc or Encs) are used to draw attention to the fact that an item
should be included with the main document. This alerts the person preparing the
mail to check that the item(s) is actually enclosed, and also the person receiving
the correspondence to check that the enclosure(s) has actually been included. If an
enclosure is found to be missing, appropriate action can then be taken.

The enclosure mark is usually placed at the end of a letter or memo with one clear
line space above and below it.

Exercise 18A

18.1 Key in the following letter, following the line spacing shown. Look back at the letter you completed in Unit 11 to refresh your memory about the parts of a letter:

Our Ref: ASL/your initials

(Today's date)

FOR THE ATTENTION OF ALL STUDENTS

Word Processing Section
The Northern College
Green Lane
NORTOWN NN3 1XZ

Dr. Student

FULLY-BLOCKED LETTER   *fully-blocked*

This is an example of a letter w. open punctuation ~~with~~ including a subject heading above this paragraph.

The term 'fully-blocked' means that each ~~every~~ line begins at ✓ the left margin. The term 'open punctuation' means that punctuation is used only in the body of the ~~document~~ letter. W___ P___ examinations demand a high standard of accuracy.

Yours scly.   *leave at least 4 clear lines here for a signature*

AS Lavedriver
Lecturer in W___ P___

18.2 Save your work – use the filename **EX18A**.

Exercise 18B

18.3 Unless it is already on your screen, recall the letter from the previous exercise: **EX18A**. Insert the following information at the appropriate places:

> (Insert as second para)
>
> ↓
>
> Letters often incorporate a small 3-column display. Start the first column at the left margin. Leave an equal number of spaces, eg 3 after the longest line in each column and set tab stops to mark the beginning of ~~second~~ & third columns.
>
> (the)

```
RSA WP Stage I often follows this pattern:

TASK 1    Letter with display     RECALL
TASK 2    Amended article         RECALL
TASK 3    Manuscript article      KEY IN
TASK 4    Passage to proofread    RECALL
```
} Insert as para 3

18.4 Save and print your work – use the same filename **EX18A** (replace the old file).

Exercise 18C

18.5 Starting with a clear screen, key in the following letter:

```
Our ref   CAL/your initials




Dear Sirs

COMPANY CALENDAR

Further to our telephone conversation of yesterday,
I am writing to confirm the details of the negatives
which were omitted from the pack of materials which
you recently returned to us.

I would be obliged if you could let me have these
negatives at the earliest opportunity so that we may
begin production of your calendar.

Yours faithfully



C A Lumiere
```

18.6 Save your work – use the filename **EX18C** (you do not need to print your work at this stage).

Exercise 18D

18.7 Recall the letter stored as EX18C. Address it to Mr S Wells Wells Welding Co Wilmer St. HALIFAX HX1 1SQ. Please insert the following information at the appropriate places.

second para
```
The negative numbers, month and view depicted are
given below:

221    January      Limoges
225    March        Bergerac
228    September     Angouleme
229    November      Libourne
```

last para

I will get in touch w. you again in approx. one month's time so that you can check the proof copies. If these are satisfactory to you, we will begin printing. ~~Pleas~~ Please let us know at this time the exact number you require.

18.8 Save and print your work – use the same filename **EX18C** (replace the old file).

18.9 Exit the program if you have finished working or continue straight on to the next unit.

At the end of Unit 19 you will have learned how to rearrange text to a specified layout.

Rearranging text in a document

One of the most useful facilities of word processing is the ability to rearrange text on the screen and then print out when all the changes have been made. The first draft is sent to the author of the text who marks up the print-out to show what changes are needed. The word-processor operator can recall the document from disk, process the text and then print out the final copy.

Rearrangement of text is tested in the RSA Stage I Word Processing examination. You have already learnt in previous units how to insert, delete and amend portions of text. In this unit you will practise how to rearrange text from one place to another within a document.

Exercise 19A

19.1 Key in the following:

```
JOBS IN THE FUTURE

In the working world of the future there will be fewer jobs
for people who have no skills at all.

Skills are special abilities, for which training is needed.
Some people have particular aptitudes in certain skills and
therefore find them easy to learn.

Jobs involving the use of simple tools and machinery are
disappearing as production processes become more advanced.

Technical and technological skills are needed in the
workplace.  It is important that workers are versatile and
adaptable and able to solve problems.

Paper work is being replaced by the use of electronic storage
mechanisms.  Office work has changed radically over the past
10 years or so with the advent of computers.  Secretaries and
clerks have had to be trained to use the new technology.

A willingness to learn new skills is an important factor in
staff recruitment.  Organisations may send their staff to
colleges or training schools; sometimes the training is
carried out in the workplace.
```

19.2 Save your work – use the filename **EX19A** (you do not need to print your work at this stage).

Exercise 19B

19.3 Unless it is already on your screen, retrieve the previous exercise: **EX19A**. Amend it as shown below.

JOBS IN THE FUTURE ← *centre and underline*

(*leave 2 clear lines here*)

In the working world of the future there will be fewer jobs for people who have no skills at all.

Skills are special abilities, for which training is needed. Some people have particular aptitudes in certain skills and therefore find them easy to learn.

⌐ *Leave at least 2" for a diagram*
∟

~~Jobs involving the use of simple tools and machinery are disappearing as production processes become more advanced.~~

now

Technical and technological skills are needed/in the workplace. It is important that workers are versatile, ~~and~~ adaptable and able to solve problems.

Paper work is being replaced by the use of electronic storage mechanisms. Office work has changed radically over the past 10 years ~~or so~~ with the advent of computers. Secretaries and clerks have had to be trained to use the new technology.

A willingness to learn new skills is an important factor in staff recruitment. Organisations may send their staff to colleges or training ~~schools~~; sometimes the training is carried out in the workplace. (*Centres*)

Some people say that in the future we will spend 'less time' at work and that job-sharing and early retirement will be more common.] *Indent by ½" from both margins*

Be prepared to learn and re-learn and to acquire new skills & qualifications throughout yr. working life.

19.4 Save your work – use the same filename **EX19A** (replace the old file). You do not need to print your work at this stage.

Exercise 19C

19.5 Unless it is already on your screen, retrieve the file: **EX19A**. Move the paragraphs as shown below. Refer back to Unit 2 to refresh your memory on how to move blocks of text:

<u>JOBS IN THE FUTURE</u> ← *remove underline*

In the working world of the future there will be fewer jobs for people who have no skills at all. Skills are special abilities, for which training is needed. Some people have particular aptitudes in certain skills and therefore find them easy to learn.

return at least 2" here

Technical and technological skills are needed now in the workplace. It is important that workers are versatile, adaptable and able to solve problems.

Paperwork is being replaced by the use of electronic storage mechanisms. Office work has changed radically over the past 10 years with the advent of computers. Secretaries and clerks have had to be trained to use the new technology.

A willingness to learn new skills is an important factor in staff recruitment. Organisations may send their staff to colleges or training centres; sometimes the training is carried out in the workplace.

Some people say that in the future we will spend less time at work and that job-sharing and early retirement will be more common.

Be prepared to learn and re-learn and to acquire new skills and qualifications throughout your working life.

19.6 Save and print your work – use the same filename **EX19A** (replace the old file).

Exercise 19D

19.7 Starting with a clear screen, key in the following text. Use single-line spacing and a justified right margin:

```
GUIDE TO RECRUITMENT OF STAFF


First ask yourself whether other members of staff could share the
workload.  Is the vacancy really necy.?  A full job description
must be written for the job.  This shd. be a summary of the main
elements of the work and the job to be done.  It is a good idea
to list the tasks in order of importance.

It is important to be specific although the document need not be
a lengthy one.  An accurate job description avoids confusion
later.

In addition, you should be clear about the type of person you wd.
want for the job.  Consider age and experience as well as skills
+ qualifications.  An older person may be less likely to move on
to another job or firm than a younger one just setting out on a
career path.

Any job advert. shd. clearly show the title & a description of
its duties.  It is necy. too for the advert. to be completely
truthful - an applicant could take legal proceedings against you
if the job turned out to have been falsely presented.
```

19.8 Save your work – use the filename **EX19D** (you do not need to print your work at this stage).

Exercise 19E

19.9 Recall this work (stored as EX19D) and amend it where shown. Save under same filename and print one copy.

> Finding out about an applicant's hobbies & interests could give you ~~an~~ valuable insight into his or her character.

GUIDE TO RECRUITMENT OF STAFF ← underline

                   find out   ⌐ leave ½" clear

First ~~ask yourself~~ whether other members of staff could share the
workload.   Is   the   vacancy   really   necessary?   A full job
description must be written for the job.   This should be a
summary of the main elements of the (work) and the (job) to be done.
It is a good idea to list the tasks in order of importance.

                   very
It is/important to be specific although the document need not be
a lengthy one.   An accurate job description avoids /confusion
later.   misunderstanding and

(Indent ½" at left)

~~In addition,~~ You should be clear about the type of person you
~~would~~ want for the job. Consider age and experience as well as
skills and qualifications. An older person may be less likely
to move ~~off~~ to another job or firm than a younger one just setting
out on a career path.

                                              job
Any job advertisement should clearly show the /title and a
description of its duties.   It is necessary too for the
advertisement to be completely truthful - an applicant could take
legal proceedings against you if the job turned out to have been
falsely presented.

Application forms shd. be completed by all the applicants.
At the interview it is a good idea to make notes on this
form so that you can be certain to assess the interviewee
in the light of the requirements of the job. After
speaking to a no. of applicants, you may need to read
thro' yr. notes to refresh yr. memory before coming to
a final decision.

Task 1

Retrieve the letter stored under filename **CON21**. Delete the first address. Insert the following information where indicated. Save and print a copy of your file – use the filename **CON31**.

Please insert immediately after Yours sincerely:
ELVERTON BUS. ESTATE

Delete the third paragraph and replace with:

As we are about to undertake extensive landscaping work to the grounds of our large bus. complex, I wd. be interested to know if we could rec. any discount for bulk orders. Can you also advise us/you offer a planning service for landscaping work.
whether

Add the following text and table after the final paragraph:

In the meantime, I would like to place an order w. you for the following items:

Cat No AT NO	ITEM	QUANTITY	COST(£)
XR 421	BENCH	3 4	37.99
PL 16	TABLE	3	26.99
FN 22	PERGOLA	1	45.99

Mark the letter: For the attention of Mr Swallow

Task 2

Key in the text below. Use a justified right margin. Save and print a copy of your file – use the filename **CON32**.

BASIC FUNCTIONS OF A COMPUTER MODEL ← *(centre & bold)*

The first electronic computers were produced *(a radical ~~seria~~ series of 4)* in the 1980s. Since then we have continued to exp. ↑breakthroughs in electronics ~~an~~ as scientists seek to dev. *new & better* models to mimic human intelligence. The basic elements wh. make up a model computer are as *(fallows)*:

a) Input. Some computers cannot accept data in forms customary to human communication, *(its)* necy. to present data to the c_____ in a way wh. provides easy conversion into *(it's)* own electronic pulse-based forms.

b) Control. Each c_____ has a control unit which *(fetched)* instructions from ~~the~~ main storage, interprets them & issues signals to / ^all the components making up the model. *(where they are)*

c) Storage. Data & instructions *(~~are entered~~)* enter main storage ~~and~~ held ~~is~~ until needed to be worked on.

d) Computer/processing. Instructions are obeyed and the necy. arithmetic operations etc are carried out on the data.

(Indent 5 spaces at left and right margins)

The arithmetic-logical unit, control unit and main storage combine to form the Central Processing Unit (CPU). The C___ P___ U___ is often ~~thus~~ referred to as *(bieng)* the "brain" of the computer.

(double-line spacing for this paragraph)

Task 3

Retrieve the document stored under filename **CON32**. Amend where shown. Save and print a copy of your file – use the filename **CON33**.

BASIC FUNCTIONS OF A COMPUTER MODEL

leave at least 1" space here for a photo

~~The first electronic computers were produced in the 1940s. Since then~~ We have continued to experience a radical series of breakthroughs in electronics as scientists seek to develop ~~new and~~ better models to mimic human intelligence.

The basic elements which make up a computer model are as follows:

a) Input. Since computers cannot accept data forms customary to human communication, it is necessary to present data to the computer in a way which provides easy conversion into its own electronic pulse-based forms.

b̸) / c Control. Each computer has a control unit which fetches instructions from main storage, interprets them and issues signals to all the components making up the model.

c̸) / b Storage. Data and instructions enter main storage where they are held until needed to be worked on.

d) Computer/processing. Instructions are obeyed and the necessary arithmetic operations etc are carried out on the data.

The arithmetic-logical unit, control unit and main storage combine to form the <u>Central Processing Unit</u> (CPU). The Central Processing Unit is often referred to as being the "brain" of the computer.

Main storage is supplemented by less costly backing storage (eg disks) for mass storage purposes.

e) Output Results are taken (form) mains storage & fed to an output device (eg Printer)

Operator: * Use some form of emphasis for all words underlined with ⌇
* change right margin to ragged
* alter line length of document to 54
* remove left and right indent of the enumerated paragraphs a)–e) so that they become aligned flush with the left margin
* search for and replace the word model(s) with system(s)

Printing-out arrangements in the RSA Stage I Examination

In this examination, each task should fit on one page of A4 paper.

You are given six sheets of A4 plain paper in this examination. This is sufficient paper to be able to print out *two draft copies* during the examination time, leaving *four sheets* for the final copies of each task. No additional stationery is allowed.

During the examination, you may use a calculator, a dictionary, the program's spellchecker and a program instruction manual which has been prepared by the centre.

The printing of the final copies of the tasks in this examination may be done outside the examination time of one and a half hours *by the invigilator or by the candidate*.

Make sure that you always save your work under the filename given so that the correct documents for printing can be easily located on your disk.

Printing is closely supervised. No amendments may be made to the text after the examination time has expired, and printing is usually therefore done from the directory or list of files.

The invigilator at your examination centre will explain the procedures to be followed for printing in that centre.

Task 1

Retrieve the letter stored under filename: **CORE1**. Delete the first address, mark the letter **URGENT** and insert the following information where indicated. Save under the same filename and print one copy. You may use either a justified or a ragged margin:

Insert this paragraph at the end of the fourth paragraph

The sweatshirt colours would be burgundy, green & white with black and white logo. (Please see the enclosed drawings for colour & design details.) We would require the sweatshirts in the following sizes, styles and quantities:

SIZE	STYLE	QUANTITY
26-28/30-32	Crew-neck	850
34-36/38-40	V-neck	700
40-42	V-neck	400

This table to be inserted as details of sweatshirt requirements

Please insert immediately after Yours sincerely

FRIENDS OF NATURE SOCIETY

Task 2

Key in the details below. Choose either a justified or ragged margin. Save and print a copy of your file – use the filename **FROGS**:

FRIENDS OF NATURE   – FROGS + TOADS   *(leave at least 6 clear line spaces here)*

In Britain the number of Natterjack toads has declined drastically since the fifties.

The Natterjack is recognised by its short back legs, thin yellow lines, warty skin and silver-gold eyes (down the greenish back)

Man has, ~~over the years,~~ interfered with the toad's natural habitat by ~~going~~ increasingly encroaching into sand dune areas, building holiday camps in such places, draining sandy heathlands, starting careless fires and draining ponds.   *(use double-line spacing for this paragraph)*

The ecological consequences of removing such vast numbers of frogs is causing great concern.

Sadly, numerous toads die each yr. crossing busy roads to reach their ~~breeding~~ areas. [Lately, however, volunteers have become resp. for operating patrols to see the toads across safely e there are even road signs ~~posted at intervals along the way~~ to highlight major crossing points.

The F__ O_ N__ Society recom. everyone to help frogs and toads by making a garden pond. You shd. include the following necy. features:

(indent 10 spaces from left margin)

a) shallow water (less than 12") for frogs to spawn in e deeper areas (up to 24") for toads

b) rocks e stones at the edges to give froglets and toadlets easy exits

c) water plants for food and cover and to provide temp. support for toad spawn.

It wd. be essential, of course, to keep the pond free from fish, ducks etc

Task 3

Retrieve the document stored under filename **FROGS**. Amend where shown and change to a justified right margin. Save and print a copy of your file – use the filename **FROGS2**:

FRIENDS OF NATURE - FROGS AND TOADS ← *underline and centre*

leave 3 clear line spaces only here

In Britain the number of Natterjack toads has declined drastically since the fifties. The Natterjack is recognised by its short back legs, thin yellow line down the greenish back, warty skin and silver-gold eyes. *It is a nocturnal amphibian wh. makes a vibrating noise that has been compared with a 2-stroke motorbike reputed to have been heard over half-a-mile away.*

~~Man has interfered with the toads natural habitat by encroaching increasingly into sand dune areas, building holiday camps in such places, draining sandy heathlands, starting careless fires and draining ponds.~~

indent at least 1" from left and right margins

Sadly, ~~numerous~~ *many* toads die each year crossing busy roads to reach their breeding areas.

Lately, however, *teams of* volunteers have become responsible for operating patrols to see the toads safely across and there are even road signs to highlight major crossing points.

The growing trend for garden ponds has provided new havens and breeding sites for frogs and toads and the more common species are staging a remarkable comeback.

The Friends Of Nature Society recommend everyone to help frogs and toads by making a garden pond. You should *also* include the following ~~necessary~~ features

  a) shallow water (less than 12") for frogs to spawn in and deeper areas (up to 24") for toads

  b) rocks and stones at the edges to give froglets and toadlets easy exits

  c) water plants for food and cover and to provide temporary support for toadspawn.

It would be essential, of course, to keep the pond free from fish, ducks etc.

unit 21   *RSA Stage I word-processing mock assignment*

Task 4

Key in the following document correcting the errors circled and following the amendments. Save and print a copy of your file – use the filename **FROGS3**:

THE INDIAN BULLFROG ← Spaced capitals and bold

The Indian Bulfrog (Rana tigrina) is one of the most common species of frog found in India. the species is found manely in the ditches and marshes of the Nepal Valley and at the base of the Himalayas. During the warm season it becomes nocturnal and passed the days sitting in a concealed cavity in the earth.

Milions of frogs are slaughtered each year to meet a growing demand to provide the gourmet delicacy of frogs legs for European restaurants. and American

An adult frog consumes approcximatly its own weight in insects' every day. It is feared that the removal of vast numbers of these frog could lead to a significant increase in the pest population.

Exercise 1A

Your name

INTRODUCTION TO WORD PROCESSING

Word Processing is sometimes called Text Processing but the latter term is usually used to cover not only Word Processing but also Typewriting and Audio Transcription.

This book has been designed to allow you (the student) to achieve the skills to be successful in RSA (Royal Society of Arts) examinations.

You can work at your own pace at home, in a school or college, or at work. Print-out checks are provided at the back of the book so that you can be sure your work is correct before you go on to the next unit. Don't forget to use them. It is recommended that you work through the book step by step so that your skills and knowledge increase and develop in a logical manner.

Before commencing a Word Processing course, it is important that you can use a QWERTY keyboard well. Learning the correct fingering methods first means that you will later be able to become a fast and accurate Word Processor operator. This book is designed for use with any Word Processing program and space has been left at relevant points for the insertion of the specific program commands. Refer to your Manufacturer's manual or your tutor for help.

Exercise 2A

Your name

INTRODUCTION TO WORD PROCESSING

Word Processing is sometimes called Text Processing but the latter term is usually used to cover not only Word Processing but also Typewriting and Audio Transcription.

Word Processing is not only an updated method of producing documents. It is more than an extension of typewriting. Nowadays many executives and administrators do their own word processing so that they can compose on to the screen and produce perfect copy in a short time.

This book has been designed to allow you (the student) to achieve the skills to be successful in RSA examinations.

Before commencing a Word Processing course, it is important that you can use a QWERTY keyboard well. Learning the correct fingering methods first means that you will later be able to become a fast and accurate Word Processor operator. This book is designed for use with any Word Processing program and space has been left at relevant points for the insertion of the specific program commands. Refer to your Manufacturer's manual or your tutor for help.

You can work at your own pace at home, in a school or college, or at work. Print-out checks are provided at the back of the book so that you can be sure your work is correct before you go on to the next unit. Don't forget to use them. It is recommended that you work through the book step by step so that your skills and knowledge increase and develop in a logical manner.

INTRODUCTION TO WORD PROCESSING

Exercise 3A

Your name

INTRODUCTION TO WORD PROCESSING

Word Processing is sometimes called Text Processing but the latter term is usually used to cover not only Word Processing but also Typewriting and Audio Transcription.

Word Processing is not only an updated method of producing documents. It is more than an extension of typewriting.

Nowadays many executives and administrators do their own word processing so that they can compose on to the screen and produce perfect copy in a short time.

This book has been designed to allow you (the student) to achieve the skills to be successful in RSA examinations. Before commencing a Word Processing course, it is important that you can use a QWERTY keyboard well. Learning the correct fingering methods first means that you will later be able to become a fast and accurate Word Processor operator. This book is designed for use with any Word Processing program and space has been left at relevant points for the insertion of the specific program commands. Refer to your Manufacturer's manual or your tutor for help.

You can work at your own pace at home, in a school or college, or at work. Print-out checks are provided at the back of the book so that you can be sure your work is correct before you go on to the next unit. Don't forget to use them. It is recommended that you work through the book step by step so that your skills and knowledge increase and develop in a logical manner.

INTRODUCTION TO WORD PROCESSING

Exercise 3B

Your name

INTRODUCTION TO WORD PROCESSING

Word Processing is sometimes called Text Processing but the latter term is usually used to cover not only Word Processing but also Typewriting and Audio Transcription.

Word Processing is not only an updated method of producing documents. It is more than an extension of typewriting.

Nowadays many executives and administrators do their own word processing so that they can compose on to the screen and produce perfect copy in a short time.

This book has been designed to allow you (the student) to achieve the skills to be successful in RSA examinations. Before commencing a Word Processing course, it is important that you can use a QWERTY keyboard well. Learning the correct fingering methods first means that you will later be able to become a fast and accurate Word Processor operator. This book is designed for use with any Word Processing program and space has been left at relevant points for the insertion of the specific program commands. Refer to your Manufacturer's manual or your tutor for help.

You can work at your own pace at home, in a school or college, or at work. Print-out checks are provided at the back of the book so that you can be sure your work is correct before you go on to the next unit. Don't forget to use them. It is recommended that you work through the book step by step so that your skills and knowledge increase and develop in a logical manner.

INTRODUCTION TO WORD PROCESSING

Exercise 4C

SALE OF RENAULT 18 SALOON CAR

With reference to your enquiry about the sale of my Renault 18 saloon vehicle which I received yesterday, I can supply you with the following details:

The registration number is C476 TWR. The colour is Metallic Blue. The engine has a 1600 cubic capacity.

The vehicle is taxed for 6 months and has a 12-month MOT certificate. All the bodywork is in excellent condition. The vehicle has been garage maintained and serviced regularly from new.

Exercise 5B

LYNDHURST HOTEL

MENU

Soup of the Day
Melon & Grape Cocktail
Egg Mayonnaise

Roast Dinner of the Day
Salmon Hollandaise
Courgette Bake
Chicken Kashmir

Lyndhurst Chocolate Gateau
Fresh Fruit Salad
Apple Charlotte
Selection of Local Cheeses

Coffee & Mints served in Lounge Area

Exercise 5D

TEXT PROCESSING HINTS

UNDERSTANDING THE DRAFT COPY

HANDWRITING - make sure you can **read all the words** written in longhand. If any words are not clear, **look for the same** letter formations in other parts of the draft where they may be more legible. If you still have difficulty, read the document for **context** to try to get the sense of it.

CORRECTIONS - make yourself familiar with the standard correction and amendment signs.

ABBREVIATIONS - make yourself familiar with the standard abbreviation signs. Remember, there are some abbreviations such as **etc** or **eg** which should remain in their abbreviated form.

Exercise 6A

TEXT PROCESSING

In addition to editing facilities, text formatting can be
carried out. Editing includes the insertion and deletion of
text from single characters to large paragraphs.

Formatting features include the facilities for changing the
line spacing and the margins and altering the format in which
the text is presented.

One example of changing the format is switching from a ragged
right margin to a justified right margin or vice versa.

An efficient operator would key in the text fairly quickly and
then proof-read the work and correct any errors. At the same
time, decisions can be made about the best way of setting out
the work for maximum effect. A text editor is very much
concerned with potential readers of the finished document and
should try to use effective presentation techniques so that
the author's intended message is transmitted as simply and
clearly as possible.

Exercise 6B

TEXT PROCESSING

In addition to text editing facilities, word
processors also allow text formatting to be carried
out. Editing includes the insertion and deletion of
text from single characters to large paragraphs.

Formatting features include the facilities for
changing the line spacing and the margins and altering
the format in which the text is presented.

Emboldening, underlining, changing line spacing and
margins are methods of making words, sentences or
paragraphs stand out from the remainder of the text.
Emphasis draws the reader's attention to key points.

An efficient operator would key in the text fairly
quickly and then very carefully proof-read the work
and correct any errors. At the same time, decisions
can be made about the best way of setting out the work
for maximum effect. A text editor is very much
concerned with potential readers of the finished
document and should try to use effective presentation
techniques so that the author's intended message is
transmitted as simply and clearly as possible.

Exercise 6C

MORE WORD PROCESSING TERMINOLOGY

A word processor operator talks to the computer through its keys.

The operator gives instructions to the computer in the form of commands. These commands are given at the appropriate point when text is being keyed in or being edited. For example, before typing an underlined heading, the operator will insert a command to begin underlining: at the end of the heading, another command is inserted to stop underlining. Because the commands are 'set into' the text, they are called EMBEDDED COMMANDS.

Many large organisations use the MAILMERGE or MAILSHOT capability of a word processor. The names and addresses of customers are stored as one file: a standard letter is stored as another file. The two files are merged at the time of printing and each customer receives a letter which appears to have been individually prepared for them.

Some people think that this facility has been over-used recently as it has resulted in a large increase in unsolicited 'junk mail'.

Exercise 6D

MORE WORD PROCESSING TERMINOLOGY

The word processor operator gives instructions to the computer in the form of commands. These commands are given at the appropriate point when text is being keyed in or being edited. Because the commands are 'set into' the text, they are called EMBEDDED COMMANDS or CODES.

Many large organisations use the MAILMERGE or MAILSHOT capability of a word processor. The names and addresses of customers are stored as one file: a standard letter is stored as another file. The two files are merged at the time of printing and each customer receives a letter which appears to have been individually prepared for them.

Some people think that this latter facility has been used far too much recently as it has resulted in a large increase in unsolicited 'junk mail'.

However, most employers and office workers would agree that word processing is a much more effective and interesting use of the human resource than bashing away on a manual typewriter and re-typing the whole document each time a change is required.

Unit 7
Print-out 1

FIRST AID - RESUSCITATION

Resuscitation should be attempted even if you are unsure
whether a patient is capable of being revived. You should
always continue until: spontaneous breathing and pulse are
restored; someone else comes along to help; a doctor takes
over; or you are exhausted. It is easiest to carry out if the
patient is lying on the back but it should be started
immediately whatever the position the patient is in.

In order to find out whether a patient is breathing, place
your ear above the patient's mouth to see if you can feel
their breath on your face. Also, watch for movement along the
chest and abdomen.

To give mouth-to-mouth ventilation you blow air from your
lungs into the patient's mouth or nose. The air you breathe
out contains about 16% oxygen. This is more than is needed to
sustain life. When you take your mouth away, the patient
should breathe out.

You should not give mouth-to-mouth ventilation if there is any
contamination from poisoning around the patient's mouth, if
there are serious facial injuries or if there is recurrent
vomiting.

Print-out 2

FIRST AID - RESUSCITATION

Resuscitation should be attempted even if you are
unsure whether a patient is capable of being revived.

You should always continue until: spontaneous
breathing and pulse are restored; another person takes
over; a doctor takes over; or you are exhausted. It
is easiest to carry out if the patient is lying on the
back but it should be started immediately whatever the
position the patient is in.

In order to find out whether a patient is breathing,
place your ear above the patient's mouth to see if you
can feel their breath on your face. Also, watch for
movement along the chest and abdomen.

You should also be able to observe changes in the
patient's colour - when the patient is not breathing
properly the face and lip colour is blue (cyanosis).

To give mouth-to-mouth ventilation you blow air from
your lungs into the patient's mouth or nose. The air
you breathe out into the patient's lungs contains
about 16% oxygen. When you take your mouth away, the
patient should breathe out.

Exercise 9B

CORE TEXT PROCESSING MARKING SCHEME

The work of candidates in the above examinations is assessed under three headings - production rate, accuracy, and presentation. Each criterion must be satisfied for a pass or a distinction to be awarded.

Production rate is the ability to complete the three tasks within the one hour allowed.

Accuracy is the ability to produce work which is error-free. A word missing or a word which is superfluous counts as one error.

Presentation refers to the appearance of the document, eg use of paper size, line spacing, clean and uncreased copy.

A D V E R T I S I N G

We do not realise how much we are affected by advertisements in our everyday lives. Large companies employ specialists from a separate firm to advise and prepare their campaigns. An advertising agency will recommend the best type of advertisement and, if required, will be responsible for the whole process right through to presentation of the finished video, film, display, or newspaper page.

A business which is just being set up will definitely find it necessary to advertise its products or services widely if it is to be a success. There are many inexpensive methods which give a small business the opportunity to publicise itself - for example, printed paper bags, posters or handbills.

Exercise 9D

P R O O F R E A D I N G   Y O U R   W O R K

In text processing examinations, candidates are often expected to be able to find any errors which appear in the copy and to make sure that all these errors have been corrected in their final typewritten or printed work.

At elementary and intermediate levels, any such errors are circled and the typist simply has to identify what is wrong and put it right.

It is very important to check all your work before you take it out of your typewriter, or before you print out if you are using a word processor.

METHODS OF ENHANCING TEXT

The most commonly used methods are bold and underline.

The Core Text Processing Skills examination may be taken on a typewriter or a word processor. Your typewriter could be a manual one, an electric one or an electronic one. Manual and electric typewriters are not usually able to produce emboldened text so the main method of emphasis is underlining.

Word processors also allow the 'font' to be changed so that the characters vary in size and appearance. Sophisticated programs which are often expensive to buy, offer a wide choice of typestyle.

Exercise 9E

ABBREVIATIONS

Core Text Processing Skills examinations contain abbreviations

which have to be reproduced in full and correctly spelt. The

days of the week should always be typed in full and with a

capital letter at the beginning, eg Thurs. should be Thursday,

Wed. should be Wednesday.

In addition, the months of the year should be expanded eg Jan.

should be January, Feb. should be February, Oct. should be

October.

In addresses, Crescent, Drive, Avenue, Grove should be typed

in full. Other examples are Road for Rd., Street for St.

Many students make mistakes when typing the complimentary

close at the end of a letter. Yours always has a capital

letter but sincerely, faithfully and truly begin with a small

letter.

Abbreviations are always written with a full stop after them.

This is to be omitted, of course, when typed in full.

Exercise 10B

FOLLOWING MANUSCRIPT COPY

When you have to type from a page of manuscript copy, first
read it through carefully. Clarify any words, figures and
abbreviations which are not immediately clear by looking
elsewhere in the draft for the same letter formations.

Reading the draft for meaning will also help you to interpret
any illegible words.

Pay careful attention to editing – look out for text which has
been crossed out and therefore should not be keyed in and also
for text which needs to be inserted at marked points. It can
sometimes be easy to mistake a comma for a full stop.

Because handwriting takes up more room than typescript you
will have to judge the finished layout of the draft, set
suitable margins and make your own line-endings (or allow
wordwrap to do so).

LANGUAGE SKILLS IN TEXT PROCESSING

A good knowledge of English is very important because the copy
which is given to the word processor operator will not be
'perfect'. It may be in any of the following forms:

manuscript
typescript
dictated onto audio-tape
dictated and written in shorthand.

More often than not, it will be necessary for the operator to
make amendments and corrections to the original draft. Some
of the amendments and corrections will be clearly identified
but others may be questionable, and this is where the
operator's language skills become vital.

A wide vocabulary and knowledge of the subject matter will be
of great assistance and an understanding of grammar and
punctuation will help the operator, and eventually the reader,
to interpret the writer's message correctly.

You should develop your language skills by reading a wide
variety of materials and by learning about the business or
industry in which you are involved. If you are learning word
processing as a student, you will also be acquiring a
business-based vocabulary through the text which you work with
and the other subjects in your programme.

Exercise 11B

74 Richmond Road
Wellerton Park
BRADFORD
BD19 2JS

Today's date

Mr A Sykes
Home Decorating Services Ltd
21-23 Alton Street
LEEDS
LS1 2BY

Dear Mr Sykes

With reference to your recent advertisement in the Daily News, would you please arrange to call at my address and let me have an estimate for decorating 3 bedrooms and a kitchen.

I would be grateful if you could bring with you any colour charts, wallpaper samples and paint ranges etc which could be of interest to me and which you would recommend.

I shall be glad if you will confirm that your business if definitely reliable and that you would be able to carry out the work sometime in February when I shall be on holiday and my accommodation will be empty.

You can contact me through my secretary at my company office on telephone no. 93-653168 any time during working hours.

Yours sincerely

M Davies (Miss)

Unit 12
Task 1

26 Lister Avenue
SHEFFIELD
SH2 3GS

today's date

Mr S Swallow
26 Foster Street
LOOE
Cornwall
LO5 BR2

Dear Mr Swallow

Thank you for your letter, along with brochure and price list of garden equipment, seeds, bulbs and shrubs which I received last week.

I am definitely interested in your range of pergolas and garden furniture which I believe you have on special offer until the end of the year.

As I am part of a large gardening society I would be interested to know if you could offer any discounts for bulk orders and the quantities it would be necessary to order before discount was available.

I am also anxious to purchase a shrub entitled 'Kalmia latifolia' which is not shown in your current brochure and wonder if you can recommend another supplier of this item.

Yours sincerely

R Thomas (Miss)

Task 3

THE HUMAN TORSO

The human torso is made up of millions and millions of cells which sometimes work singly (as in the case of the white cells of the blood) but more often, when they are concerned in carrying out the same kind of function, are grouped together in what are called organs such as the heart, liver, kidneys and so on.

The skeleton, with the muscles attached to its separate bones and covered by the skin and its appendages, gives the torso its characteristic appearance and supports the whole structure. Inside the skull and backbone, or spine, and protected by them are the brain and spinal cord.

Connecting these parts and making possible communications between them and the rest of the body are the nerves. There is a very close connection between the nervous system and the muscles, and because life is largely maintained by movements of all kinds these two are often spoken of as the master tissues of the torso.

Task 4

THE HUMAN BODY

The human body is made up of millions and millions of cells which sometimes work singly (as in the case of the white cells of the blood) but more often, when they are concerned in carrying out the same kind of function, are grouped together in what are called organs such as the heart, liver, kidneys and so on.

When two or more organs are grouped together

to serve some special function, such a group

is spoken of as a system; we have, for

example, the circulatory, the respiratory,

the digestive and reproductive systems.

The skeleton, with the muscles attached to its separate bones and covered by the skin and its appendages, gives the body its characteristic appearance and supports the whole structure. Inside the skull and backbone, or spine, and protected by them are the brain and spinal cord.

Connecting these parts and making possible communications between them and the rest of the body are the nerves. There is a very close connection between the nervous system and the muscles, and because life is largely maintained by movements of all kinds these two are often spoken of as the master tissues of the body.

THE HUMAN BODY

Unit 13
Task 1

14 Fairview Road
BOLTON
BT4 5RM

Today's date

Mr B West
Betterbuy Products
23 Park Street
KEIGHLEY
KH9 2AP

Dear Mr West

Thank you for sending your brochure and price list of novelties and fancy goods.

I am secretary of the local Friends of Nature Society and we are interested in purchasing some of your goods for our fund-raising campaign.

We would like to know if it would be possible to have our Society logo engraved on some of your goods. It is a beaver in a circle with the words "Friends of Nature" going round the outer edge.

We would be particularly interested in the range of tailor-made sweatshirts you have on offer, providing the logo could definitely be printed on these garments.

I look forward to your reply.

Yours sincerely

V Lambert (Mrs)

Task 2

Mr B West
Betterbuy Products
23 Park Street
KEIGHLEY
KH9 2AP

Task 3

NATURE'S ARCHITECTS

Animals use a wide variety of materials in building their homes. The structures are often complex, ingenious and sometimes enormous in scale.

As its name implies, the paper wasp uses a paper-like material which it produces itself by chewing wood.

Weaver ants 'sew' leaves together. After the thread has been silk-spun by the ant larva, it is passed back and forth from one leaf to another, gripped between the jaws of an adult ant.

Honey bees make their combs from wax that is formed in flakes underneath the worker bees' abdomens. This honeycombed pattern of the wasps nest is strong, yet light, and has been copied in the design of some aircraft wings.

Termite towers are made from mud mixed with the saliva of termites - a mixture which sets hard as concrete.

Exercise 14

```
EASYCLEAN SALES - JULY

HALIFAX    145  125  176  110  145  126
LEEDS      105  158  169  145  128  177
DEWSBURY   180  140  150  145  126  110
```

Exercise 16A

INTRODUCING COMPUTERS

1   ELECTRONIC: The machine uses thousands of microscopic electronic components which can fit on to a single silicon microchip (smaller than the size of a finger nail).

2   PROGRAMMABLE: Once an instruction is given the machine will carry out the task by itself – without the instruction it is unable to operate.

3   INFORMATION PROCESSORS: Information is input into the computer (by people or machines) then processed in the computer and then output by the computer (by people or machines).

Exercise 16B

TEXT PROCESSING HINTS

UNDERSTANDING THE DRAFT COPY

HANDWRITING – make sure you can **read all the words** written in longhand. If any words are not clear, **look for the same letter formations** in other parts of the draft where they may be more legible. If you still have difficulty, read the document for **context** to try to get the sense of it.

CORRECTIONS – make yourself familiar with the standard **correction** and **amendment** signs.

ABBREVIATIONS – make yourself familiar with the standard abbreviation signs. Remember, there are some abbreviations such as **etc** or **eg** which should **remain** in their abbreviated form.

```
STOCK NO   DESCRIPTION                          SALE PRICE (£)

DEV356     Green corduroy pleated skirt             12.99
TYR359     Blue denim shirt                         17.99
CRT47      Yellow double-breasted silk blouse       26.99
ZXW35      Brown sweatshirt top                     14.99
```

Exercise 16C

SALE OF RENAULT 18 SALOON CAR

With reference to your enquiry about the sale of my Renault 18 saloon car which I received yesterday, I can supply you with the following details:

The registration number is C476 TWR. The colour is Metallic Blue. The engine has a 1600 cubic capacity.

The vehicle is taxed for 6 months and has a 12-month MOT certificate. All the bodywork is in excellent condition. The car has been garage maintained and serviced regularly from new.

```
JOB VACANCIES

Job No   Department        Job Description

58       Main Reception    Receptionist/Telephonist
59       Accounts          Junior Clerk
60       Marketing         Shorthand-Typist
```

Exercise 17B

DISK OPERATING SYSTEM

DOS is the abbreviated name for Disk Operating System. The system allows many functions to be carried out:

It is possible to see a list of all the files on a disk (the directory). Files may be deleted from this directory by using a simple command at the C or A prompt.

Disks are copied and formatted through DOS. Formatting makes a disk ready to accept data. It is possible to copy a file from one disk to another, or copy the whole contents of a disk.

The directory (example above) can be printed out on paper then this can be kept in the disk envelope as a quick reference to the disk's contents.

The Disk Operating System is used to make back-up copies of disks and files. These should be kept in a safe place and regularly up-dated.

Exercise 17A

THE FIRS WOODLANDS AVENUE

The Firs is an imposing Victorian house set in attractive, mature gardens of approximately 1 acre. It was built in 1857 for Jonas Appleyard, a local mill owner, to house his large family and its servants.

The property has spectacular, panoramic views to the south over the valley.

The accommodation briefly comprises on the ground floor: entrance hall, 3 reception rooms, large kitchen, scullery, pantry and lavatory.

The accommodation on the first floor comprises: 4 double bedrooms, 1 with en-suite bath/shower room, 1 box room, and a large family bathroom.

There are extensive cellars as is usual in houses of this age and type. To the south-west of the house, with access from the dining room, is an attractive hexagonal conservatory of timber construction with feature leaded lights.

For further details, please contact our Halifax office.

Exercise 18A

Our Ref: ASL/your initials

Date of Typing

FOR THE ATTENTION OF ALL STUDENTS

Word Processing Section
The Northern College
Green Lane
NORTOWN
NN3 1XZ

Dear Student

FULLY-BLOCKED LETTER

This is an example of a fully-blocked letter with open
punctuation including a subject heading above this paragraph.
The term 'fully-blocked' means that every line begins at the
left margin. The term 'open punctuation' means that
punctuation is used only in the body of the letter.

Letters often incorporate a small 3-column display. Start the
first column at the left margin. Leave an equal number of
spaces, eg 3 after the longest line in each column and set tab
stops to mark the beginning of the second and third columns.

RSA WP Stage I often follows this pattern:

TASK 1   Letter with display   RECALL
TASK 2   Amended article   RECALL
TASK 3   Manuscript article   KEY IN
TASK 4   Passage to proofread   RECALL

Word processing examinations demand a high standard of
accuracy.

Yours sincerely

A S Lavedriver
Lecturer in Word Processing

Exercise 18C

Our ref CAL/your initials

Date of typing

Mr S Wells
Wells Welding Co
Wilmer Street
HALIFAX
HX1 1SQ

Dear Sirs

COMPANY CALENDAR

Further to our telephone conversation of yesterday, I am
writing to confirm the details of the negatives which were
omitted from the pack of materials which you recently returned
to us.

The negative numbers, months and view depicted are given
below:

221   January   Limoges
225   March   Bergerac
228   September   Angouleme
229   November   Libourne

I would be obliged if you could let me have these negatives at
the earliest opportunity so that we may begin production of
your calendar.

I will get in touch with you again in approximately one
month's time so that you can check the proof copies. If these
are satisfactory to you, we will begin printing. Please let
us know at this time the exact number you require.

Yours faithfully

C A Lumiere

Exercise 19A

JOBS IN THE FUTURE

In the working world of the future there will be fewer jobs for people who have no skills at all. Skills are special abilities, for which training is needed. Some people have particular aptitudes in certain skills and therefore find them easy to learn.

A willingness to learn new skills is an important factor in staff recruitment. Organisations may send their staff to colleges or training centres; sometimes the training is carried out in the workplace.

Be prepared to learn and re-learn and to acquire new skills and qualifications throughout your working life.

Some people say that in the future we will spend less time at work and that job-sharing and early retirement will be more common.

Technical and technological skills are needed now in the workplace. It is important that workers are versatile, adaptable and able to solve problems. Paperwork is being replaced by the use of electronic storage mechanisms. Office work has changed radically over the past 10 years with the advent of computers. Secretaries and clerks have had to be trained to use the new technology.

Exercise 19D

GUIDE TO RECRUITMENT OF STAFF

First find out whether other members of staff could share the workload. Is the vacancy really necessary?

A full job description must be written for the job. This should be a summary of the main elements of the job and the work to be done. It is a good idea to list the tasks in order of importance.

It is very important to be specific although the document need not be a lengthy one. An accurate job description avoids misunderstanding and confusion later.

Any job advertisement should clearly show the job title and a description of its duties. It is necessary too for the advertisement to be completely truthful – an applicant could take legal proceedings against you if the job turned out to have been falsely presented.

Finding out about an applicant's hobbies and interests could give you valuable insight into his or her character.

You should be clear about the type of person you want for the job. Consider age and experience as well as skills and qualifications. An older person may be less likely to move to another job or firm than a younger one just setting out on a career path.

Application forms should be completed by all the applicants. At the interview it is a good idea to make notes on this form so that you can be certain to assess the interviewee in the light of the requirements of the job. After speaking to a number of applicants, you may need to read through your notes to refresh your memory before coming to a final decision.

Unit 20
Task 1

For the attention of Mr Swallow

today's date

Mr S Swallow
26 Foster Street
LOOE
Cornwall
LO5 BR2

Dear Mr Swallow

Thank you for your letter, along with brochure and price list of garden equipment, seeds, bulbs and shrubs which I received last week.

I am definitely interested in your range of pergolas and garden furniture which I believe you have on special offer until the end of the year.

As we are about to undertake extensive landscaping work to the grounds of our large business complex, I would be interested to know if we could receive any discount for bulk orders. Can you also advise whether you offer a planning service for landscaping work.

I am also anxious to purchase a shrub entitled 'Kalmia latifolia', which is not shown in your current brochure and wonder if you can recommend another supplier of this item.

In the meantime, I would like to place an order with you for the following items:

CAT NO	ITEM	QUANTITY	COST (£)
XR421	BENCH	4	26.99
PL16	TABLE	3	37.99
FN22	PERGOLA	1	45.99

Yours sincerely
ELVERTON BUSINESS ESTATE

R Thomas (Miss)

Task 2

BASIC FUNCTIONS OF A COMPUTER MODEL

The first electronic computers were produced in the 1940s. Since then we have continued to experience a radical series of breakthroughs in electronics as scientists seek to develop new and better models to mimic human intelligence.

The basic elements which make up a computer model are as follows:

a) Input. Since computers cannot accept data in forms customary to human communication, it's necessary to present data to the computer in a way which provides easy conversion into its own electronic pulse-based forms.

b) Control. Each computer has a control unit which fetches instructions from main storage, interprets them and issues signals to all the components making up the model.

c) Storage. Data and instructions enter main storage where they are held until needed to be worked on.

d) Computer/processing. Instructions are obeyed and the necessary arithmetic operations etc are carried out on the data.

The arithmetic-logical unit, control unit and main storage combine to form the Central Processing Unit (CPU). The Central Processing unit is often referred to as being the "brain" of the computer.

Unit 21
Task 1

Today's date

URGENT

Mr B West
Betterbuy Products
23 Park Street
KEIGHLEY
KH9 2AP

Dear Mr West

Thank you for sending your brochure and price list of novelties and fancy goods.

I am secretary of the local Friends of Nature Society and we are interested in purchasing some of your goods for our fund-raising campaign.

We would like to know if it would be possible to have our Society logo engraved on some of your goods. It is a beaver in a circle with the words "Friends of Nature" going round the outer edge.

We would be particularly interested in the range of tailor-made sweatshirts you have on offer, providing the logo could definitely be printed on these garments. The sweatshirt colours would be burgundy, green and white with black and white logo. (Please see enclosed drawings for colour and design details.) We would require the sweatshirts in the following sizes, styles and quantities:

SIZE	STYLE	QUANTITY
26-28/30-32	V-neck	700
34-36/38-40	Crew-neck	850
40-42	V-neck	400

I look forward to your reply.

Yours sincerely
FRIENDS OF NATURE SOCIETY

V Lambert (Mrs)

Encs

Task 3

BASIC FUNCTIONS OF A COMPUTER SYSTEM

We have continued to experience a radical series of breakthroughs in electronics as scientists seek to develop better systems to mimic human intelligence.

The basic elements which make up a computer system are as follows:

a) Input. Since computers cannot accept data forms customary to human communication, it is necessary to present data to the computer in a way which provides easy conversion into its own electronic pulse-based forms.

b) Storage. Data and instructions enter main storage where they are held until needed to be worked on. Main storage is supplemented by less costly backing storage (eg disks) for mass storage purposes.

c) Control. Each computer has a control unit which fetches instructions from main storage, interprets them and issues signals to all the components making up the system.

d) Computer/processing. Instructions are obeyed and the necessary arithmetic operations etc are carried out on the data.

e) Output. Results are taken from main storage and fed to an output device (eg Printer).

The arithmetic-logical unit, control unit and main

storage combine to form the Central Processing Unit

(CPU). The Central Processing Unit is often referred

to as being the "brain" of the computer.

Task 2

FRIENDS OF NATURE - FROGS AND TOADS

In Britain the number of Natterjack toads has declined drastically since the fifties. The Natterjack is recognised by its short back legs, thin yellow line down the greenish back, warty skin and silver-gold eyes.

Man has interfered with the toad's natural habitat by

encroaching increasingly into sand dune areas, building

holiday camps in such places, draining sandy heathlands,

starting careless fires and draining ponds.

Sadly, numerous toads die each year crossing busy roads to reach their breeding areas.

Lately, however, volunteers have become responsible for operating patrols to see the toads safely across and there are even road signs to highlight major crossing points.

The Friends Of Nature Society recommend everyone to help frogs and toads by making a garden pond. You should include the following necessary features:

a) shallow water (less than 12") for frogs to spawn in and deeper areas (up to 24") for toads

b) rocks and stones at the edges to give froglets and toadlets easy exits

c) water plants for food and cover and to provide temporary support for toadspawn.

It would be essential, of course, to keep the pond free from fish, ducks etc.

Task 3

FRIENDS OF NATURE - FROGS AND TOADS

In Britain the number of Natterjack toads has declined drastically since the fifties. The Natterjack is recognised by its short back legs, thin yellow line down the greenish back, warty skin and silver-gold eyes. It is a nocturnal amphibian which makes a vibrating noise that has been compared with a 2-stroke motorbike reputed to have been heard over half-a-mile away.

Sadly, many toads die each year crossing busy roads to reach their breeding areas.

Lately, however, teams of volunteers have become responsible for operating patrols to see the toads safely across and there are even road signs to highlight major crossing points.

The growing trend for garden ponds has provided new havens and breeding sites for frogs and toads and the more common species are staging a remarkable comeback.

The Friends Of Nature Society recommend everyone to help frogs and toads by making a garden pond. It would be essential, of course, to keep the pond free from fish, ducks etc. You should also include the following features:

a) shallow water (less than 12") for frogs to spawn in and deeper areas (up to 24") for toads

b) rocks and stones at the edges to give froglets and toadlets easy exits

c) water plants for food and cover and to provide temporary support for toadspawn.

Task 4

THE INDIAN BULLFROG

The Indian Bullfrog (Rana tigrina) is one of the most common species of frog found in India. The species is found mainly in the marshes and ditches of the Nepal Valley and at the base of the Himalayas. During the warm season it becomes nocturnal and passes the days sitting in a concealed cavity in the earth.

Millions of frogs are slaughtered each year to meet a growing demand to provide the gourmet delicacy of frogs legs for European and American restaurants.

An adult frog consumes approximately its own weight in insects every day. It is feared that the removal of vast numbers of these frogs could lead to a significant increase in the pest population.

Unit	Topic	Date completed	No. of errors
1	Load the WP program		
	Select correct disk drive		
	Create a new document/file		
	Key in text		
	Move cursor around document		
	Edit text (delete/insert)		
	Split/join paragraphs		
	Save work to disk		
	Print work		
	Clear the screen		
	Exit the WP program		
2	Retrieve a file from disk		
	Shade a block of text		
	Delete a block of text		
	Restore deleted text		
	Move a block of text		
	Copy a block of text		
3	Ragged right margin		
	Justified right margin		
	Inset left margin		
	Inset right margin		
	Double-line spacing		
	View document before printing		
4	Search and replace text		
	Spellcheck a document		
5	Emboldening text		
	Underlining text		
	Centring text		

Unit	Topic	Date completed	No. of errors
6	Consolidation 1		
7	RSA CLAIT mock assignment		
8	Unfamiliar/foreign words		
9	Typescript containing: correction signs		
	abbreviations		
	typographical errors		
	errors of agreement		
10	Typing from manuscript copy		
	Additional correction signs		
11	Personal business letters		
	Insert a new page marker		
	Envelopes		
12	Consolidation 2		
13	Core text mock examination		
14	Tabulation		
15	RSA I abbreviations		
16	Indent key		
	Alter document line length		
17	Allocate vertical space		
	Confirm facts		
18	Business letters		
	Special marks		
	Enclosure marks		
19	Rearrange text		
20	Consolidation 3		
21	RSA Stage I mock examination		